BLESSING YOUR HUSBAND

BLESSING *Your* HUSBAND

Understanding and Affirming Your Man

Debra Evans

Tyndale House Publishers, Inc.
Carol Stream, Illinois

ISBN-13: 978-1-58997-478-4

A Focus on the Family Book published by Tyndale House Publishers, Inc.
Carol Stream, Illinois 60188

Focus on the Family and the accompanying logo and design are federally registered trademarks of Focus on the Family, Colorado Springs, CO 80995.

TYNDALE and Tyndale's quill logo are registered trademarks of Tyndale House Publishers, Inc.

Library of Congress Cataloging-in-Publication Data
Evans, Debra.
  Blessing your husband / Debra Evans.
     p. cm.
Includes bibliographical references.
  ISBN 1-58997-003-9
  1. Wives—Religious life. 2. Husbands—Religious life. 3. Marriage--Religious aspects—Christianity. 4. Man-woman relationships—Religious aspects—Christianity. I. Title.
BV4528.15 .E93 2003
248.8'435—dc21

                                                            2003001798

Editor: Erin Healy
Project Manager: Kathy Davis
Cover photograph of couple copyright © by Aldomurillo/iStockphoto. All rights reserved.
Cover background texture copyright © by Mammuth/iStockphoto. All rights reserved.
Cover border texture copyright © by Kativ/iStockphoto. All rights reserved.
Cover design by Ron Kaufmann

Printed in the United States of America
1 2 3 4 5 6 7 8 9 / 13 12 11 10 09

ALSO BY DEBRA EVANS

The Complete Book on Childbirth
The Mystery of Womanhood
Heart & Home
Fragrant Offerings
Beauty for Ashes
Without Moral Limits
Blessed Events
Preparing for Childbirth
The Woman's Complete Guide to Personal Health Care
Beauty and the Best
Christian Parenting Answers (General Editor)
Women of Character
Kindred Hearts
Ready or Not, You're a Grandparent
The Christian Woman's Guide to Sexuality
The Christian Woman's Guide to Personal Health Care
Women of Courage
The Christian Woman's Guide to Childbirth
Without Moral Limits (Revised Edition)
Soul Satisfaction
Blessing Your Grown Children

For David

❖

CONTENTS

Let all that you do be done in love.
—1 CORINTHIANS 16:14, NASB

❦

The development of a really good marriage isn't a natural process. It's an achievement.
—DAVID AND VERA MACE

INTRODUCTION

If anyone was ever entitled to be served by other people, Jesus was. But think about how He treated his closest companions: He got out a towel and started scrubbing their feet. Why?

"God sees us with the eyes of a Father," asserts author and minister Max Lucado. "He sees our defects, errors, and blemishes. But he also sees our value. What did Jesus know that enabled him to do what he did? Here's part of the answer. He knew the value of people. He knew that each human being is a treasure. And because he did, people were not a source of stress but a source of joy."[1]

In marriage, most of us are willing enough to serve—if our spouse is equally willing, that is. When our husband lets us down, keeping our mind on marital ministry can be more difficult. But foot washing, not bookkeeping, is the first order of business on our personal agenda, especially where our marriages are concerned: "Be completely humble and gentle; be patient, bearing with one another in love. Make every effort to keep the unity of the Spirit through the bond of peace" (Ephesians 4:2-3).

Completely humble? *Every* effort? That's a tall order, and one I'll be spending more time on over the course of this book. Until then, however, let me give you a snapshot to refer to in the event you are wondering, "What does the biblical concept of blessing actually mean, and what does it have to do with my marriage?"

Family counselors Gary Smalley and John Trent, authors of *The Blessing*, offer the following explanation:

> Genuine acceptance radiates from the concept of the blessing. For sons and daughters in biblical times, receiving their father's blessing was a momentous event. At a specific point in their lives they would hear words of encouragement, love, and acceptance from their parents. [Some] aspects of this Old Testament blessing were unique to that time. However, the relationship elements of this blessing are still applicable today. In Old

Testament times, this blessing was primarily reserved for one special occasion. In contrast, [family members] today can decide to build these elements of blessing into [one another's] lives daily....[2]

Ephesians 2:4-10 gives us a small glimpse of blessing's definition in the matchless blessing our Father bestowed on us through His Son:

> But because of his great love for us, God, who is rich in mercy, made us alive with Christ even when we were dead in transgressions—it is by grace you have been saved. And God raised us up with Christ and seated us with him in the heavenly realms in Christ Jesus, in order that in the coming ages he might show the incomparable riches of his grace, expressed in his kindness to us in Christ Jesus. For it is by grace you have been saved, through faith—and this not from yourselves, it is the gift of God—not by works, so that no one can boast. For we are God's workmanship, created in Christ Jesus to do good works, which God prepared in advance for us to do.

Talk about *blessing!* Words can't begin to describe the fullness of blessing God has bestowed upon us by His grace: Our debt has been canceled; God has made us alive with Christ! And that is the basis for the blessings we bestow on our husband.

In the following chapters, I want to help you nurture your understanding of the many ways in which you can bless your husband. As your understanding increases, so will your capacity for putting your God-given gifts to use for His glory. Jesus calls each of us to use what the Father gives us (see Matthew 25:14-30; Ephesians 2:10). When we do, we invest valuable treasure where it can never be taken away from us—no matter what tomorrow brings.

In the meantime, as St. Augustine advised, "Do what you can do, and pray for what you cannot do." Although our exclusive, committed love for our husband can't come close to approximating the Lord's unfailing love for him, God asks us to partner with Him in blessing our husband on His behalf.

Blessing our husband conveys our approval of him, thereby affirming he is lovable, capable, and valuable simply because of who he is. Dr. Smalley and Dr. Trent suggest that blessings include meaningful touch, spoken messages, attaching high value to those we bless, and picturing a special future for them.[3] In each case we base the blessing on our commitment to seeing God's blessings in their lives come to pass. We bless our husband, for example:

- by our words and actions, by way of our prayers, through our body language, with our facial expressions and physical gestures, and in the tone of our voice
- with nurturing touch and loving caresses as we welcome him with our body
- when we give him gifts, write birthday cards and notes of appreciation, make a surprise phone call in the middle of a busy workday, or extend an invitation for lunch
- through sending him spoken and unspoken messages that honor and encourage his God-given position of spiritual leadership, side-by-side ministry, and sacrificial service within marriage

By blessing our husband and holding him up in prayer before our loving Father, we quietly exercise the privilege of participating in the work of heaven. Blessing our husband for our Father's glory—investing time, prayer, and tender loving care on our husband's behalf—is an essential means of home and kingdom building that brings lasting rewards: "For God is not unrighteous to forget your work and labour of love, which ye have shewed toward his name, in that ye have ministered to the saints, and do minister" (Hebrews 6:10, KJV). Additionally, blessing our husband:

- enables us to "do what we can do" even as we lift our unmet needs, innermost desires, and private concerns to God
- turns our eyes toward the solution for the helplessness we feel when God asks us to abandon our well-meaning but futile attempts to direct, lead, steer, or otherwise reroute our husband's life
- helps us walk with our husband through his defeats and triumphs in the strength of God's grace as we depend on the Holy Spirit's timely guidance and assistance

- teaches us the wisdom of waiting, listening, and looking for God's answers to our questions and concerns regarding our husband
- leads us to our Father's protective pastures for the Shepherd's safekeeping, the only place where we unfailingly find trouble-free rest for our souls

Jesus modeled the concept of blessing for His disciples when He broke bread with them, cooked fish for them, and spoke of His Father's love and purposes for them. Jesus lived to do the will of His Father; He did not function independently but maintained the vital connection with His Father in heaven. In Christ's active and obedient ministry to others, we have a perfect example of the kind of active love on which the good work of blessing our husband is based.

By deciding to read *Blessing Your Husband*, you have expressed a desire to strengthen the bond you share with your husband. You honor the commitment you made on that memorable day when your lives were joined together in Christ. You recognize the importance of your role as a wife and realize, as I do, that this consecrated union is the most influential, exclusive, revealing, meaningful, and humbling relationship in your life. Whether you have been married for days or years, you understand that your words, actions, attitudes, and prayers have a big impact on your husband, your heart, and your marriage. It's my hope that you'll receive an ample dose of encouragement as you read this book and spend time thinking about ways to fortify the vital connection you share with your spouse.

I stand with you in your effort! I did not write *Blessing Your Husband* because I think I have all the answers (does anyone?) or because I can claim that my thirty-seven years of wifely experience have been completely free of stress, strain, and disappointment. I wrote these pages because I want to, as loudly and clearly as I can, cheer you on toward reinforcing, valuing, and protecting your marriage bond. I want to affirm the eternal worth of your wifely role, and to ever so gently remind you that a successful, meaningful marriage *is* possible if you aren't afraid to ask God repeatedly for His help, strength, mercy, and wisdom.

It is my hope that this book will provide you with the tools you need to grow closer to God and to your husband. Each chapter ends with several reflection and action points, and I urge you to set aside focused time as you can—perhaps weekly—with these:

- Focus Points—summaries of the most important points from each chapter for quick review.
- Words to Remember—scriptures to live by and meditate upon as you spend time with the Lord.
- Real Guys—thoughts from husbands about what their wife does that truly blesses them.
- Personal Reflections—questions and journal exercises to help you think more deeply and personally about how certain principles apply to your marriage.
- Prayers—adapted from Scripture and from the classics to assist you as you pray for your husband and your marriage. You might consider copying these onto index cards and placing them strategically in your purse, bathroom, kitchen, car, office, or wherever you will see them often.
- Blessings Now—collected ideas from which you can choose simple blessings to begin extending to your husband today.
- For Further Reading—a recommended reading list of books that will take you deeper into the issues discussed in each chapter. While the Christian books on this list are excellent in my opinion, they represent a variety of perspectives, so focus on those that are personally helpful to you in your efforts to strengthen your marriage. Out-of-print books can often be located through libraries, used bookstores, and online booksellers.

As we place Jesus above all other relationships and personal interests, we receive the grace to grow up into Christ as well as into our marriage—to increasingly surrender our biases, self-centeredness, and scorekeeping. In doing so, we experience the freedom that allows us to bless our husband not only with wisdom, but also with dignity and joy.

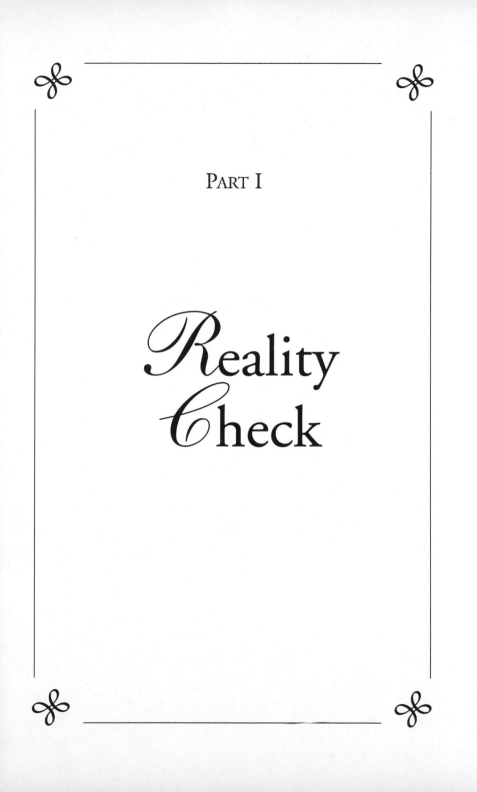

PART I

Reality Check

ONE

Married Outside of Eden

❧

*Marriage is not simply the luck of the draw, or
something that we get involved in which just
unfolds before us like a long movie.
Good marriages, like good individual lives or good art,
are conscious creations. They are made.*

KEVIN AND MARILYN RYAN

*D*o you sometimes wish you could once and for all insulate your marriage from failure and frustration, that you could shock-proof your sacred bond? Do you ever long for spiritual shortcuts on the road to holiness together?

Our easily distracted human heart seeks the easy detours. Whether living our life or loving our husband, we prefer wide, paved roads to the rugged, step-by-step path that requires us to continually seek and submit to God's will, pray about everything, get help when we need it, thank God for *all* He has done, and travel on.

But marriage, of course, isn't a smoothly paved, predictable journey; it's a bumpy love-in-action relationship filled with disorienting roadside challenges and constant surprises. Wedded life requires strenuous, open-hearted endurance—a continuing, conscious effort to remain obedient to

God's transforming work in our life—over hundreds of months and thousands of days. A healthy marriage can't be built *immediately*, but it *can* be built. Couples committed to creating one must carefully construct and cement their bond, layer by layer.

Arduous Demands and Astonishing Surprises

"The divine design is no mistake," writes Gladys Hunt, author of *Ms. Means Myself.* "The mutual attraction of male and female calls us to confront our aloneness, out of our independence to see that we need each other. It is the foundation of human history. We are meant to enhance each other, to affirm the other's personhood and to discover that in our mutual dependence we solve the mystery of our existence."[1]

The exclusive intimacy marriage requires is obviously part of God's plan for us. Even so, loving our husband—*genuinely* loving him accord-

❀ ❀ ❀ ────────────────────────────────

The Truth about Marriage

Marriage is the closest bond that is possible between two human beings. That, at least, was the original idea behind it. It was to be something unique, without parallel or precedent. In the sheer sweep and radical abandon of its commitment, it was to transcend every other form of human union on earth, every other covenant that could possibly be made between two people. Friendship, parent-child, master-pupil—marriage would surpass all these other bonds in a whole constellation of remarkable ways, including equality of the partners, permanent commitment, cohabitation, sexual relations, and the spontaneous creation of blood ties through simple spoken promises. As it was originally designed, marriage was a union to end all unions, the very last word, and the first, in human intimacy. Socially, legally, physically, emotionally, every which way, there is just no other means of getting closer to another human being, and never has been, than in marriage.

Such extraordinary closeness is bought at a cost, and the cost is nothing

ing to the way love is defined in the New Testament—doesn't come naturally for any of us. When our husband disagrees with us, offends us, or annoys us, our desire to continuously care for and cherish him is challenged. This, too, is part of God's plan for us: learning what love is, and what it's not, within the incredibly instructive context of marriage.

"Scriptures give us careful, meticulous descriptions of the many aspects of love," Stuart and Jill Briscoe point out in *Living Love*. "It's important to take a close look at the sixteen descriptions of love in 1 Corinthians 13:4-7 and not get sidetracked when reading it simply because it is so familiar or so beautiful. There are rugged, abrasive qualities in this passage that describe what love really is when it is in operation.... Love is not primarily something that you feel. You cannot love with God's love, merely by oohing and aaahing over the 'love chapter.' The Scriptures require action."[2]

Marriage is full of staggering wonder and risk, incomprehensible

---

more or less than one's own self. No one has ever married without being shocked at the enormity of this price and the monstrous inconvenience of this thing called intimacy which suddenly invades their life.... All of life is, in one way or another, humbling. But there is nothing like the experience of being humbled by another person, and by the same person day in and day out. It can be exhausting, unnerving, infuriating, disintegrating. There is no suffering like the suffering involved in being close to another person. But neither is there any joy nor any real comfort at all outside of intimacy, outside the joy and comfort that are wrung out like wine from the crush and ferment of two lives being pressed together....

The truth about marriage is that it is a way not of avoiding any of the painful trials and subtractions of life, but rather of confronting them, of exposing and tackling them most intimately, most humanly. It is a way to meet suffering personally, head on, with the peculiar directness, the reckless candidness characteristic only of love. It is a way of living life with no other strategy or defense or protection than that of love.... Marriage is a way not to evade suffering, but to suffer purposefully.[3]—Mike Mason

⚘ ⚘ ⚘

mystery and surprise, unique joys and sorrows. Over the course of a marriage, life can be amazingly serene at certain moments, completely exasperating at others. Given the imperfect, fallen world we live in, every day we face the startling possibility that we will experience the effects of sin, loss, and disappointment. As Eve's daughters, our marriage makes its way outside of Eden.

The apostle Paul expressed this reality well when he wrote, "We know that the whole creation has been groaning as in the pains of childbirth right up to the present time" (Romans 8:22). What a powerful statement! As a veteran childbirth educator and the mother of four children, my heart almost skips a beat when I read this Bible passage. *The whole creation has been groaning as in the pains of childbirth as it awaits its final redemption from the effects of the Fall*—and it still is. Can you hear the groaning?

Though it's easy on difficult days to forget our ultimate goal, our labor and our groans are deeply productive where God's eternal purpose for us is concerned: "For our light and momentary troubles are achieving for us an eternal glory that far outweighs them all. So we fix our eyes not on what is seen, but on what is unseen. For what is seen is temporary, but what is unseen is eternal" (2 Corinthians 4:17-18).

The Real Task at Hand

Do you believe God is productively and perfectly working for the good of your marriage, for your husband, and for you? Do you daily trust God to shape and design your husband's life—and also your own?

I don't know about you, but when I experience frustration or anger regarding my husband's attitudes or actions, I usually slip into Control Mode. I tend to cope with both big and small concerns about my spouse by subtly (or not so subtly) attempting to redirect, reorganize, and redecorate him. When things start getting messy, I want to straighten up my husband's life.

For example, when David drives too fast, I tend to sigh loudly, raise my eyebrows in disapproval, and point out the obvious speed limit signs. Even though I know my tendency will fail to transform his driving, I would like to spare both of us the embarrassment and expense of a traffic citation. It's hard for me not to say anything to my husband, even though one well-timed speeding ticket would have a far greater effect on David's driving than all my sighs, eyebrow raising, and finger pointing combined. As you can imagine, this same principle applics to any number of areas of our life together.

I realize my behavior seems fairly ridiculous. After all, what educated woman treats her husband as if he were a continuing interior design challenge? I can't help but think that if Eve had been completely content with Adam, God, and herself, she might never have presumed to eat the forbidden fruit, nor would she have offered "just a tiny bite" to her husband.

Perhaps you, too, see the problem. This age-old behavior pattern concerning husband improvement is, I suspect, something I share with many women, including my famous foremother from the Garden of Eden.

Regardless of how much we love our husband, we will dislike certain things about him, as he will dislike certain things about us. If we lay down our desire to control, however, and open our heart to see our husband as he really is rather than focusing on who we want him to be, our ability to love and forgive and bless him will grow. When we accept the responsibility of understanding and appreciating our husband's uniqueness—the sum total of his singular spiritual, physical, psychological, and social attributes—our focus remains where it belongs: on God, and on His unchanging purposes and promises for our marriage, our husband, and ourself.

The inconstant world where we negotiate our *en route* existence is not what it once was, nor what it will one day be. Life, like labor, is full of arduous demands and astonishing surprises. We live in a physically, emotionally, and spiritually trying environment that C. S. Lewis, the inspired British writer and philosopher, called "the shadowlands." Our daily pilgrimage unfolds in a varied landscape of not-yet-fully illuminated places that continually challenge us to go deeper, go further, with God. If we rise to the challenge, we can expect to see and understand better His life-giving, glorious reality.

FOCUS POINTS

- Wedded life requires a continuing, conscious effort to remain obedient to God's transforming work in our life. God is productively and perfectly working for the good of your marriage, for your husband, and for you.
- Given the imperfect, fallen world we live in, every day we face the startling possibility that we will experience the effects of sin, loss, and disappointment. But our labor and our groans are deeply productive where God's eternal purpose for us is concerned.
- If we lay down our desire to control our husband—if we open our heart to see him as he really is rather than focusing on who we want him to be—our ability to love and forgive and bless him will grow.
- When we accept the responsibility of understanding and appreciating our husband's uniqueness, our attention remains where it belongs: on God and on His unchanging purposes and promises for our marriage, our husband, and ourself.

WORDS TO REMEMBER

- The Lord is faithful to all his promises and loving toward all he has made. (Psalm 145:13)
- Be very careful, then, how you live—not as unwise but as wise, making the most of every opportunity, because the days are evil. Therefore do not be foolish, but understand what the Lord's will is. (Ephesians 5:15-17)
- Your hands made me and formed me; give me understanding to learn your commands. (Psalm 119:73)
- Be imitators of God, therefore, as dearly loved children. (Ephesians 5:1)

REAL GUYS

"Kind, helpful, and unselfish actions always lift my spirits emotionally, spiritually, and even physically. But one thing transcends the attention focused upon me. I have heard friends of my wife comment, 'What a great husband you have!' Others tell me directly,

'What a wonderful relationship you and your wife must have.' You see, it's not only that she has done something to me to be a blessing, but that she has acknowledged to other people the blessing of what we have together."—Jim

PERSONAL REFLECTIONS

1. At what point in your marriage, if ever, do you first remember thinking, "This is harder than I thought it was going to be"? How did God help you keep going? What have you learned along the way?
2. Complete these thoughts in your journal:
   The destination we're aiming for in our marriage is...
   On difficult days, it helps to remember...
   God met me at a point of need in my marriage when...
3. If you're currently struggling with an annoying character trait or habit that's really bugging you about your husband and it's clear he isn't interested in making a change right now, what will you do to relieve your feelings of anger, hurt, or frustration? Record your thoughts and feelings and prayers—for your eyes only.

PRAYERS

Praying God's Blessing for Our Marriage*
God, be gracious to us and bless us and make your face shine upon us, that your ways may be known on earth, your salvation among all nations.—Psalm 67:1-2
Praying God's Blessing for My Husband*
God of peace, who through the blood of the eternal covenant brought back from the dead our Lord Jesus, that great Shepherd of the sheep, equip my husband with every good thing for doing your will, and may you work in my husband what is pleasing to you, through Jesus Christ, to whom be glory for ever and ever. Amen.—Hebrews 13:20-21
Closing Prayer
O God of patience and consolation, give us such goodwill, we beseech Thee, that with free hearts we may love and serve Thee and our brethren; and, having thus the mind of Christ, may begin heaven

on earth, and exercise ourselves therein till that day when heaven where love abideth shall seem no strange habitation to us. For Jesus Christ's sake. Amen.[4]—Christina G. Rossetti (1830-1895)

*Pronouns in all end-of-chapter prayers for blessing are personalized.

BLESSINGS NOW

- Open your heart to seeing your husband as he is in his Father's eyes rather than thinking about who you want him to be.
- Nurture emotional as well as physical intimacy. Touch your husband while silently praying for his physical, emotional, and spiritual well-being.
- Admit it when you realize you're wrong: "Therefore confess your sins to each other and pray for each other so that you may be healed" (James 5:16).
- For at least one day, set aside thoughts of your husband's faults or shortcomings. Focus instead on God's unchanging promises and purposes for him.
- Try to understand your husband's opinion during a disagreement or dispute. Aim to make allowances for the differences between you.
- Extend grace in place of negative criticism: Identify one thing about your husband that really bugs you and decide from this day forward you will avoid trying to change this particular behavior.
- Encourage your partner to play. Ask him what he would like to do with his evening, then help protect his time by taking his phone calls and limiting interruptions.
- Avoid taking your husband for granted today. Express your appreciation for your beloved by putting your love into action on his behalf in some noticeable, new way.
- Slow down. Savor a quiet moment together behind closed doors.
- Boldly go where no woman has gone before: Invite your husband to imagine a future with you in which you picture growing old together. Talk about your hopes, dreams, and fears about turning 30 . . . 40 . . . 50 . . . 60 . . . 70 and beyond.

FOR FURTHER READING

Dietrich Bonhoeffer. *Life Together.* New York: Harper & Brothers, 1954.

Stuart and Jill Briscoe. *Living Love.* Wheaton, Ill.: Harold Shaw, 1993.

Charles Colson and Nancy Pearcey. *How Now Shall We Live?* Wheaton, Ill.: Tyndale, 1998.

Larry Crabb. *The Marriage Builder.* Grand Rapids: Zondervan, 1982, 1992.

James Dobson. *Love for a Lifetime.* Sisters, Ore.: Mult-nomah/Questar, 1993.

Bill and Lynne Hybels. *Fit to Be Tied.* Grand Rapids: Zondervan, 1991.

Al Janssen. *The Marriage Masterpiece.* Wheaton, Ill.: Tyndale, 2001.

Donald M. Joy. *Bonding: Relationships in the Image of God.* Waco, Tex.: Word, 1985.

C. S. Lewis. *Mere Christianity.* New York: Macmillan, 1943.

Mike Mason. *The Mystery of Marriage.* Portland, Ore.: Multnomah, 1985.

Gary Smalley and John Trent. *The Gift of the Blessing.* Nashville: Thomas Nelson, 1993.

John R. W. Stott. *Christian Counter-Culture: The Message of the Sermon on the Mount.* Downers Grove, Ill.: InterVarsity Press, 1978.

Charles Swindoll. *Strike the Original Match.* Wheaton, Ill.: Tyndale, 1990.

Gary Thomas. *Sacred Marriage.* Grand Rapids: Zondervan, 2000.

TouchPoints for Couples: God's Answers for Your Daily Needs. Wheaton, Ill.: Tyndale, 2000.

Walter Trobisch. *I Married You.* New York: Harper & Row, 1971.

Walter Wangerin. *As for Me and My House: Crafting Your Marriage to Last.* Nashville: Thomas Nelson, 1987.

Two

The Only Love We Have

❧

Peace and union are the most necessary of all things for men who live in common, and nothing serves so well to establish and maintain them as the forbearing charity whereby we put up with one another's defects.
Robert Bellarmine (1542-1621)

Have you ever wished you could love your husband more easily? Have you ever reached that place of brokenness where you suddenly realize how inadequate you are to really *love*?

We have married our husband with the expectation of making the journey of life together, shoulder to shoulder, hand in hand, through thick and thin, no matter where the road takes us—"to have and to hold, from this day forward, for better for worse, for richer for poorer, in sickness and health, to love and to cherish, till death us do part." That we marry believing such an enduring covenant is even possible in this day and age testifies to the God-created desire we carry within us for both a sacred marriage and that deeper something that only the Shepherd of our souls can supply. Whether we stay the course depends on our level of reliance upon God's grace and on our daring choice to keep believing in this glorious possibility.

"If I had had any idea what I was really getting myself into when I married Mike, I might have approached our wedding day more soberly, felt a few more qualms, and been a bit more wobbly walking down the aisle," my friend Diane recently confided. "But it wouldn't have changed my decision. I love my husband more today than I ever have, and I'm more deeply aware of the power of God's healing love because of the sometimes stormy road Mike and I have traveled together. By His grace, after twenty-seven years we're still together."

Although we can't completely return to Eden's innocence, even today we can experience the remnants of Eden's glory. Perfect relationships are no longer possible this side of heaven. At one time or another, *all* couples face marriage-related feelings of helplessness, discouragement, frustration, anger, or fatigue. For only in fantasy can

✤ ✤ ✤ ————————————————————————————————

We Marry the Other One Whole

For these two reasons—that it is total and timeless—marriage is marvelous and holy; that's why we marry with a glad, almost unspeakable excitement. We surround the event with ceremony. Breathlessly we appeal unto God for a blessing. We invite more friends than we thought we had; they celebrate with us. We act differently now than we usually do, and no one blames us because this thing is so different from common human experience. Even people of an unremarkable faith will feel the need of a "church" wedding, and gruff men cry for happiness.

Yet, that isn't the whole of our feelings up against the wedding, is it? Grown men also tremble, don't they? And women lock themselves in bathrooms.

We approach the wedding with fear, and it isn't just stage fright that weakens our knees. No, some come to the speaking and hearing of this covenant plain afraid. Why is that? Is it right or common?

Most common. And perhaps it can't be helped. Look again at the two characteristics that make this contract unique—total commitment, timeless commitment—and realize that they occur within a world which is sinful and time-bound. The environment of the vow makes the vow seem hazardous after all.

one expect *every* hope, *every* desire, and *every* secret longing to be fulfilled. Though what we see in movies and on television or read about
in books and magazines may falsely lead us to expect romantic bliss,
loving our husband is, by human necessity and divine design, a lifelong learning process.

"No husbands or wives can love each other with unlimited love,"
pastor Henri J. Nouwen writes in *Bread for the Journey*. "There is no
human love that is not broken somewhere. When our broken love is
the only love we have, we are easily thrown into despair, but when we
can live our broken love as a partial reflection of God's perfect, unconditional love, we can forgive one another our limitations and enjoy
together the love we have to offer."[1]

One night as I was getting ready to serve dinner—while talking on

---

My total commitment unto another includes not only my worth and
goodness, but also my weaknesses and my sinful tendencies. Will I, who fail
so often, be able to keep covenant with my spouse in all things? Do I bring
her more trouble than treasure? Moreover, what infirmities does my spouse
bring to the marriage and to me, since I get the whole mix, the good and
the bad together? Never, never did we marry just the piece of a human
being—even though it's only bits and pieces we see before the marriage. We
marry the other one whole. But always we buy the package before we can
open it....

It is only in God that we do touch the future after all, even if we cannot
know it, for God embraces in his own knowing the present and the future
together: he who is here with us now, as we begin the relationship, is also,
now, at every anniversary of that relationship until we die. He is at the
birthing of our children, blessing the event. He is at the tragedies to come
(but he's there, by virtue of his timelessness, now), supporting and consoling
us—therefore we can go forward trustingly, even to tragedies. God joins the
times for us. God comforts and enables us despite our ignorance—and to
trust absolutely in him who knows the future is as good as though we knew
the future ourselves.[2]—Walter Wangerin, Jr.

❀ ❀ ❀

the phone, putting away a few remaining groceries, hunting for an oven mitt, adding pepper to the salad, and loading the dishwasher— I heard my husband shouting.

"Deb!" he yelled. "Come quick! You've got to see this."

In a flash, my adrenaline level shot up and my heart started racing.

"Where are you? What's wrong?" I called.

"Hurry!" David answered. "I'm in the living room. You will not believe who's on TV! Hurry! You're going to miss him!"

What? He wants me to come see the TV?!

I burned my hand on a hot cookie sheet, blurted out an expletive, and then shouted in anger at David. Where had *that* come from? I was instantly chagrined. If only I had reacted differently or said something else instead.

If only I had… It's a phrase we know by heart. When stress builds or hormones flash, emotional temperatures can quickly rise to the point of combustion. Cooling down at such moments is one of the chief challenges we face as Christians—and as wives.

One's long and winding marriage journey exposes each partner to the other's best traits and worst faults. Be that as it may, marriage is providentially designed to survive many failures on both sides. "Every husband and wife will drop the ball and prove themselves fallible time and again," note Dr. Smalley and Dr. Trent. "If we are to be people of blessing, our commitment will rest on our decision to love our spouse 'in spite of.' Our love must be the kind of love that motivated our heavenly Father to bless us with His Son, in spite of the fact we didn't deserve it and because He knew we needed that blessing so much in our own lives."[3]

The conviction that a marriage must be perfect makes a marriage fragile. "When we expect perfection, we get nothing," twentieth-century theologian Francis Schaeffer often remarked. No matter how hard we try, we can't love perfectly. There are no perfect people, no perfect relationships. No exceptions.

Giving up the idea that our marriage and mate must be perfect gives our imperfect love a place to grow. By making the bold choice to thank God for the flesh-flawed man He has providentially placed in our life, we can avoid hitching a ride on the downward spiral at the point where it begins. We can refuse to join in the destructive dance of disappointment and anger that weakens, rather than reinforces, the marriage bond. Though we can't love perfectly, we can love humanly, with a heart of flesh that causes us to look to Christ and His holy Word for strength, sustenance, and direction.

"God's grace is sufficient for our weakness. Christ's worth does cover our unworthiness, and the Holy Spirit does make us effective in spite of our inadequacy," Jerry Bridges reminds us. "When we discover we are weak in ourselves, we find we are strong in Christ.... When we most despair over our inadequacy, we find the Holy Spirit giving us unusual ability. We shake our heads in amazement and say with Isaiah, 'Lord...all that we have accomplished you have done for us' (Isaiah 26:12)."[4]

Given that our broken love is the only love we have to offer our husband, perfection simply isn't part of the picture, is it? So let's be grateful that we can't do it alone, that we must depend on Jesus to express His love through us. There's just one catch, however: It's solely up to us to bring out the basin, pour the water, pick up the towel, and begin to actively, consciously, and prayerfully minister to our husband with our human love.

FOCUS POINTS

- God has placed a desire in us for both a sacred marriage and "something deeper" that only the Shepherd of our souls can supply. Whether we stay the course in marriage depends on our level of reliance upon God's grace and on our daring choice to believe in the glorious possibility that both are possible.
- Even today we can experience the remnants of Eden's glory, though we can't completely return to its innocence. As Henri Nouwen writes, "When we can live our broken love as a partial reflection of God's perfect, unconditional love, we can forgive one another our limitations and enjoy together the love we have to offer."
- The conviction that a marriage must be perfect makes a marriage fragile. Giving up the idea that our marriage and mate must be perfect gives our imperfect love a place to grow.

WORDS TO REMEMBER

- But we have this treasure in jars of clay to show that this all-surpassing power is from God and not from us. (2 Corinthians 4:7)
- So then, just as you received Christ Jesus as Lord, continue to live in him, rooted and built up in him, strengthened in the faith as you were taught, and overflowing with thankfulness. (Colossians 2:6-7)

REAL GUYS

"I've heard other guys complain about their wives nailing them for forgetting to do something, but my wife has never done that. She always lets the unimportant things slide and she never manipulates. With stuff like getting something fixed or an upcoming appointment, she writes it on the board on the refrigerator. The guys joke that she's got me trained, but I love how it allows me to relax about things."—Mick

PERSONAL REFLECTIONS

1. Consider an area of your marriage where you might need to give your husband's imperfect love a little more latitude. How might you go about giving him grace in this area?
2. Complete these thoughts in your journal:
   Perfect love is…
   Being married has most changed me by…
   When I think about God's love for my husband, I know…
3. Do you allow your own broken love to lead you to God? In what ways? If not, how could you begin?

PRAYERS

Praying God's Blessing for Our Marriage
   May we make every effort to add to our faith goodness; and to goodness, knowledge; and to knowledge, self-control; and to self-control, perseverance; and to perseverance, godliness; and to godliness, brotherly kindness; and to brotherly kindness, love.—2 Peter 1:5-7

Praying God's Blessing for My Husband
May my husband know your grace is sufficient for him, for your power is made perfect in weakness.—2 Corinthians 12:9

Closing Prayer
O God, who hast so consecrated the state of Matrimony that in it is represented the spiritual marriage and unity betwixt Christ and his Church; look mercifully upon these thy servants, that they may love, honour, and cherish each other, and so live together in faithfulness and patience, in wisdom and true godliness, that their home may be a haven of blessing and of peace; through the same Jesus Christ our Lord, who liveth and reigneth with thee and the Holy Spirit ever, one God, world without end. Amen.—*The Book of Common Prayer*

BLESSINGS NOW

- Initiate one-on-one contact: Ask your husband how he is feeling today, especially if he is tired, down, or not feeling up to par.
- Plan a day or an evening when your sole commitment is to have fun. Take care of any necessary details ahead of time. Focus on yourselves without feeling guilty.
- Refuse to engage in retaliation or self-pity if your husband says or does something thoughtless. Resist unwise responses. Remember: "Reckless words pierce like a sword, but the tongue of the wise brings healing" (Proverbs 12:18) and "Everyone should be quick to listen, slow to speak and slow to become angry" (James 1:19).
- Compose a personal love letter telling your husband what you most appreciate and admire about him.
- Accept the responsibility of understanding your husband's uniqueness. Honor his individuality in some concrete, practical way, with no strings attached:
  - ◊ Buy a book for him by his favorite author.
  - ◊ Make a list of his best qualities and read it aloud to him during dinner.
  - ◊ Frame one of his prized childhood photos and prominently display it in your home.

◊ Create a thank-you basket containing tokens of your affection, such as toiletry items, classic quotes and poems, computer accessories, gift certificates, sporting goods, Bible-study aids, handmade love coupons, used paperbacks, tools, and other hardware gadgets.

◊ Purchase tickets for a sports event, conference, or concert he wants to attend.

• Guard your heart against tearing your husband down in your thoughts and attitudes; build him up instead. Be concerned for his interests as well as your own.

• Forgive your husband his limitations. Enjoy the love he has to offer. After reading 1 Corinthians 13:4-8, get a piece of paper and write a letter to him explaining what the passage means to you in your own words, and thanking him for showing you this kind of love in his own unique way.

FOR FURTHER READING

Dan B. Allender and Tremper Longman III. *Intimate Allies.* Wheaton, Ill.: Tyndale, 1995.

Bernard of Clairvaux. *The Love of God.* James M. Houston, ed. Portland, Ore.: Multnomah, 1983.

Dietrich Bonhoeffer. *The Cost of Discipleship.* New York: Macmillan, 1959.

Brent Curtis and John Eldredge. *The Sacred Romance: Drawing Closer to the Heart of God.* Nashville: Thomas Nelson, 1997.

Debra Evans. *Soul Satisfaction: For Women Who Long for More.* Wheaton, Ill.: Crossway, 2001.

Richard J. Foster. *Celebration of Discipline.* San Francisco: Harper-Collins, 1978.

James Houston. *The Heart's Desire.* Colorado Springs: NavPress, 1996.

James Houston. *In Pursuit of Happiness: Finding Genuine Fulfillment in Life.* Colorado Springs: NavPress, 1996.

Henri J. M. Nouwen. *Bread for the Journey: A Daybook of Wisdom and Faith.* San Francisco: HarperSanFrancisco, 1997.

Eugene H. Peterson. *A Long Obedience in the Same Direction: Discipleship in an Instant Society.* Downers Grove, Ill.: InterVarsity, 1985.

John Piper. *Desiring God: Meditations of a Christian Hedonist.* Portland, Ore.: Multnomah, 1986.

Francis Schaeffer. *True Spirituality.* Wheaton, Ill.: Tyndale, 1971.

Joni Eareckson Tada. *Heaven: Your Real Home.* Grand Rapids: Zondervan, 1995.

Neil Clark Warren. *Finding Contentment: When Momentary Happiness Just Isn't Enough.* Nashville: Thomas Nelson, 1997.

Dallas Willard. *The Divine Conspiracy: Rediscovering Our Hidden Life in God.* San Francisco: HarperSanFrancisco, 1998.

Dallas Willard. *The Spirit of the Disciplines: Understanding How God Changes Lives.* San Francisco: Harper & Row, 1988.

THREE

One Perfect Husband

For your Maker is your husband—
the Lord Almighty is his name—
the Holy One of Israel is your Redeemer;
he is called the God of all the earth.
ISAIAH 54:5

*W*ith each discovery we make concerning our husband's real self—the good, the bad, and, yes, the ugly, too—we find any sugarcoated dreams and sweet romantic fantasies we might have had confronted with these all-too-true realities:

No husband can unfailingly meet his wife's needs.

No husband can entirely fulfill his wife's expectations.

No husband can realistically live up to his wife's ideals.

No husband can completely satisfy his wife's longings.

No husband can ever make his wife's dream of perfect, never-ending love come true.

When our expectations concerning our husband's love hit a brick wall, to whom will we turn for relief, hope, wisdom, and sustenance?

"The refusal to be disillusioned is the cause of much of the suffering in human life," Oswald Chambers tells us in his classic book, *My Utmost for His Highest*. "It works this way—if we love a human being and do not love God, we demand of him every perfection and every rectitude, and when we do not get it we become cruel and vindictive; we are demanding of a human being that which he or she cannot give. There is only one Being Who can satisfy the last aching abyss of the human heart, and that is the Lord Jesus Christ."[1]

As I mentioned in chapter 1, no matter how much we might like to refashion our husband into the idealized friend and lover we desire, we can't. Neither can we demand of him what he cannot give.

"It is a foolish woman who expects her husband to be to her that which only Jesus Christ Himself can be," writes Ruth Bell Graham, "always ready to forgive, totally understanding, unendingly patient, invariably tender and loving, unfailing in every area, anticipating every need, and making more than adequate provision. Such expectations put a man under an impossible strain."[2]

Who Is Your Solid Rock?

Most of us tend toward overeager impatience when it comes to growing up together within marriage. Too often we expect too much from our husband, and we expect it *right now*. We want our mate to be good, God-pleasing, productive, faith-filled, loving, Spirit-led, generous, authoritative, heroic, prayerful, responsible, patient, knowledgeable, gentle, self-controlled, sociable, manly, Christ-centered, successful, responsive, humble, Word-wise, humorous, faithful, sober-minded, fit, caring, attentive, well-groomed, kind, respectful, even-tempered, trustworthy, affectionate, sexually skillful, capable, honest, and sensitive to our needs. We want him to be a healthy, happy, and holy man of God. We restlessly yearn for him to be able to give us the love our hearts long for. (We may as well admit it would be nice if he gave us frequent, top-quality back rubs, too!)

When we look to our husband, rather than Jesus Christ, to supply the perfect, never-ending love our hearts were created for, bitterness, disillusionment, and heartbreak predictably follow. But when we turn our heart toward Christ, He transforms our longings.

In his book *Life Together,* theologian Dietrich Bonhoeffer explains why this transfer of our attention is so important:

> Human love makes itself an end in itself. It creates of itself an end, an idol which it worships, to which it must subject everything. It nurses and cultivates an ideal, it loves itself, and nothing else in the world. Spiritual love, however, comes from Jesus Christ, it serves him alone; it knows that it has no immediate access to other persons.
>
> As only Christ can speak to me in such a way that I may be saved, so others, too, can be saved only by Christ himself. This means that I must release the other person from every attempt of mine to regulate, coerce or dominate him with my love. The other person needs to retain his independence from me; to be loved for who he is, as one for whom Christ became man, died, and rose again, for whom Christ bought forgiveness of sins and eternal life. Because Christ has long since acted decisively for my brother, before I could begin to act, I must leave him his freedom to be Christ's; I must meet him only as the person that he already is in Christ's eyes.... Spiritual love recognizes the true image of the other person which he has received from Jesus Christ; the image that Jesus Christ himself embodied and would stamp on all men.
>
> Therefore, spiritual love proves itself in that everything it says and does, it commends Christ.... It will respect the line that has been drawn between him and [me] in Christ, and it will find full fellowship with him in Christ who alone binds us together.[3]

There's just no getting around it: Expecting our mate to completely meet our needs for love and security is incompatible with true Christian love. Viewing our spouse as a means to an end—namely, as the main person responsible for satisfying our innermost needs and compensating for our inadequacies—distorts the real meaning of love and threatens our marriage by placing an intolerable burden upon our partner.

"Remember, apart from Christ, we can do nothing (see John 15:5)," emphasize pastoral care experts Dr. Neil T. Anderson and Dr. Charles Mylander. "In addition, because we are in Christ we have the assurance He will meet all our needs (see Philippians 4:19). Trying to resolve our marital conflicts without our essential needs being met in Christ will eventually prove counterproductive."[4]

Distinguishing the difference between dependence and love frees our hearts, minds, and souls to steadily rely upon Christ as the source of our strength, hope, and identity. Constrained and guided by Jesus' unfailing love, we find the freedom to choose to live according to our sacred calling in obedience to God. In this way, we learn how to love and accept our husband for who he really is, allowing us to accept him as the man he already is in Christ's eyes.

God's Unchanging Promises

God is more than able to gently guide the course of our husband's life. What a critical, life-changing truth! After all, how can you or I com-

❧ ❧ ❧ ———————————————————

Our Accepting Presence

When we get married, something happens to us women that we don't expect: We become more vulnerable to pain. You don't have to be married long before you discover this reality. The pain comes from realizing that our husbands will not completely meet our love need. It is a necessary pain that if accepted, grieved over, and embraced will lead us closer together.

From boyhood, a man is conditioned to avoid failure. Just as a girl's greatest pain is centered in her relationships, a boy's greatest pain is centered in his inadequacies. A woman defines herself by her relationships, and a man defines himself by his accomplishments.... He is conditioned to believe that he is supposed to be strong, to always have the answers, to be independent, and to know the way without asking for help. Well, we women know very well that men fail us. We can do much to help them understand and grow from their failures if we break away from the pressure we put on them not to fail us.

Fairy tales like Cinderella only further complicate the relationship between a man and a woman. Through them, a girl is conditioned to

pletely know *all* the amazing things God has accomplished, is accomplishing, and will accomplish for us and for our husband? How can we grasp the full extent of *everything* God is doing behind the scenes of our life—past, present, and future—over the course of our existence?

Simply put, we can't. We *can*, however, cling to God's unchanging promise: "And we know that for those who love God all things work together for good, for those who are called according to his purpose" (Romans 8:28, ESV). Though we can't stand on the sinking sands of what our day-to-day life experiences and fluctuating emotions "say" to us about love and marriage, we *can* rely upon the unchanging truth of God's Word and the active guidance of His Holy Spirit.

Isn't it great to know that we don't have to enter into the costly commitment of marriage without God's ever-present help, strength, nourishment, and comfort? That our hope can rest securely in the Savior,

---

believe that one day a man will come into her life, that he will never fail her, and that they will live happily ever after. We must give men room to fail and always call them back to be the best they can possibly be. When we hold to the expectation that a man must succeed in every regard every time, we drive that man further from us. As you respond to your man with encouragement, forgiveness, and a firm belief in him, you will have a great impact on his life....

As women we have a unique opportunity to call the men in our lives to greatness. We do this as our nature exposes how men's natural way of being is not healthy and needs the Holy Spirit's power to transform them for intimate relationships. In our accepting presence, our men can learn to risk failure. They will find that they need to go deeper emotionally, beyond their natural anger and aggression, to meet us emotionally and find unity. They will also perceive that having great sex involves nurturing and pleasing their wives, not just satisfying themselves. They will discover that their logical thinking is valuable but also limiting at times, especially when figuring out relationships. Our relationships with men are what call them to greatness. We invite them to become the men God means for them to be.[5]—Deborah Newman

⚘ ⚘ ⚘

who without fail hears our prayers, knows our heart, and understands our fears? At the center of our marriage, we receive God's continuing invitation to daily depend on Him to meet our needs. Learning to actively depend on Christ as our source of truth and life brings refreshing sustenance to our souls—the essential nourishment our spirits require.

"Relying on God's strength and trusting His promises isn't about taking the cowardly way out," said a woman named Carol who spoke at a retreat I attended some years ago. "Not at all! It's about *perseverance*. Holding on to and trusting the amazing, unshakable truth we so often sing about—*'The steadfast love of the Lord never ceases, His mercies never come to an end; They are new every morning, new every morning; Great is Thy faithfulness, O Lord, great is Thy faithfulness!'*—requires courage when our circumstances seem to say otherwise."

Though I had sung that song many times before, Carol's encouragement was timely. As I heard other women talk openly about the marital joys and challenges they faced, I no longer thought my circumstances as a young wife and mother were very unusual. The knowledge that God was working within each one of us according to His perfect timing, for His glory and our good, comforted me. Most of all, Carol's words about perseverance encouraged me to trust God more deeply with my heart's unspoken needs. Years later, I can look back on this notable turning point in my life with a big smile, gratitude, and a sigh of relief.

Oh, how we *always* need to believe this: "The LORD's lovingkindnesses indeed never cease, for His compassions never fail. They are new every morning; great is Your faithfulness. 'The LORD is my portion,' says my soul. 'Therefore I have hope in Him.' The LORD is good to those who wait for Him, to the person who seeks Him" (Lamentations 3:22-25, NASB).

Trusting God to satisfy our innermost longings and desires is neither easy nor automatic: We learn to let go of our desire to control over a lifetime as Jesus teaches us the meaning of true love.

Yet as we grow in love under the watchful, tender care of our Good Shepherd, choosing to believe and obey His precepts, commandments, and instructions, we increasingly realize why His burden is light and His yoke easy. Resting upon the unchanging foundation of His love, our soul enjoys refreshment, peace, and strength in His quieting presence.

In acknowledging and affirming God's control over the course of our husband's choices and experiences, we can open our hands and surrender the concerns, irritations, and anxieties to which we cling. In exchange, we receive peace and grow in the wisdom learned from trusting God with our heart, our marriage, and our life. Thus, our deep yearning for perfect love—the kind of love only God can give—becomes a source of blessing and holy protection not only for us but also for our husband.

FOCUS POINTS

- No matter how much we might like to refashion our husband into the idealized friend and lover we desire, we can't. Neither can we demand of him what he cannot give.
- When we look to our husband, rather than Jesus Christ, to supply the perfect, never-ending love our hearts were created for, bitterness, disillusionment, and heartbreak predictably follow. But when we turn our heart toward Christ, He transforms our longings.
- At the center of our marriage, we receive God's continuing invitation to daily depend on Him to meet our needs. Learning to actively depend on Christ as our source of truth and life brings refreshing sustenance to our soul—the essential nourishment our spirit requires.

WORDS TO REMEMBER

- Give thanks to the LORD for his unfailing love and his wonderful deeds for men, for he satisfies the thirsty and fills the hungry with good things. (Psalm 107:8-9)
- You are my refuge and my shield; I have put my hope in your word. (Psalm 119:114)
- The LORD is my strength and my shield; my heart trusts in him, and I am helped. My heart leaps for joy and I will give thanks to him in song. (Psalm 28:7)

- Love the Lord your God with all your heart and with all your soul and with all your mind. This is the first and greatest commandment. (Matthew 22:37-38)

REAL GUYS

"My wife has never made me feel foolish for missing something. I know other guys who get a lot of flak from their wives for being 'slow to catch on.' She's always been so understanding."—Romey

PERSONAL REFLECTIONS

1. Have you had the experience of expecting your spouse to meet needs in your life that only Christ can meet? What was the result of this experience? What did you learn about yourself—and about God—during this process?
2. Complete these thoughts in your journal:
   While reading this chapter, I thought about how I sometimes expect too much from my husband, especially when it comes to...
   Right now, the words that best describe our marriage are...
   Knowing my husband will *fail me (and vice versa) helps me understand why I need...*
3. Consider a situation in your marriage when your high expectations put your husband under an impossible strain. How did he respond? What brought relief? How will you avoid similar situations in the future?

PRAYERS

Praying God's Blessing for Our Marriage

May God bless us with his grace and wonderful peace as we come to know Jesus, our God and Lord, better and better. As we know Jesus better, his divine power gives us everything we need for living a godly life. He has called us to receive his own glory and goodness! —2 Peter 1:2-3

Praying God's Blessing for My Husband

God of hope, may you fill my husband with all joy and peace as he trusts in you, so that he may overflow with hope by the power of the Holy Spirit.—Romans 15:13

Closing Prayer

Lord, make me an instrument of Your peace.
Where there is hatred let me sow love;
where there is injury, pardon;
where there is doubt, faith;
where there is despair, hope;
where there is darkness, light;
and where there is sadness, joy.
O divine Master, grant that I may not so much seek
to be understood as to understand;
to be loved as to love.
For it is in giving that we receive;
it is in pardoning that we are pardoned
and it is in dying that we are reborn to eternal life.
—Francis of Assisi (1182-1226)

BLESSINGS NOW

- Identify and examine your expectations of your husband. Write down three or four of the most unrealistic items and commit each day to abandoning them.
- Look at your mate and recall the scripture "Christ in you, the hope of glory" (Colossians 1:27). How do you see God's image most clearly reflected in your imperfect husband today?
- Celebrate your husband's childhood memories by finding or doing something he loved as a boy but hasn't experienced recently: a chocolate-dipped Dairy Queen cone, a root beer float, or a Coney Island hot dog at a drive-in restaurant; a favorite comic book, toy, movie, or TV show; a phone call or visit with his family or an old friend from his hometown.
- Ponder your husband's unique personality and temperament, his likes and dislikes, and your hopes for his future. Make peace with the person God has created, and is creating, him to be.
- Depend more fully on Jesus to supply the perfect, never-ending love your heart was created for. Think upon Christ as you awake in the morning, asking Him to direct your heart's longings regarding your husband throughout the day.

- Give your husband your accepting presence—support instead of criticism, practical help instead of simple advice, sacrificial love instead of harsh judgments—by casting aside any disapproving, demeaning, or otherwise unconstructive thoughts for at least twenty-four hours.
- Think about what it means to embrace your husband's God-made manhood as something vitally precious to you—a gift worth blessing, affirming, and celebrating in a world turned upside down by sin. Offer him compliments that reflect your high regard for his physical, intellectual, and/or spiritual capacities.
- Symbolically acknowledge and affirm God's control over the course of your husband's life choices and experiences: Write down some of the concerns, irritations, and anxieties to which you cling, tear the paper into little pieces, and permanently dispose of them after surrendering each one to God's sovereign care.
- Make a list of the qualities, talents, and attributes you most cherish and admire in your husband. Remember this list on a difficult day.
- Accept your husband as he is: If your husband isn't presently interested in discussing spiritual matters, praying with you, or regularly attending church, persist in giving the matter to God in prayer. Don't despair; keep growing.
- Affirm your husband verbally, from the heart. Here are twenty-five encouraging examples:
    ◊ I love you.
    ◊ I like the way you did that.
    ◊ I'm glad you're here with me.
    ◊ You made a wise decision.
    ◊ I want what's best for you.
    ◊ What you're doing is really interesting.
    ◊ I appreciate your understanding.
    ◊ Let me know what you need.
    ◊ I'm thankful we're together.
    ◊ I'm happy to see you!
    ◊ Nice job!

◊ I enjoy being with you and learning new things.

◊ It's okay to tell me what you need.

◊ Thank you for your help.

◊ You figured out how to do that (name specific accomplishment) really well.

◊ I highly value your opinion.

◊ Thank you for sharing your life with me.

◊ I think you're an amazing man.

◊ No one does that as well as you.

◊ I like the way you look.

◊ I love making love with you.

◊ Your needs are okay with me.

◊ I'm thinking about you today.

◊ You are completely unique.

◊ I'm glad I married you.

FOR FURTHER READING

Neil T. Anderson and Charles Mylander. *The Christ-Centered Marriage: Discovering and Enjoying Your Freedom in Christ Together.* Ventura, Calif.: Regal, 1996.

Oswald Chambers. *My Utmost for His Highest.* New York: Dodd, Mead & Co., Inc., 1935.

Henry Cloud. *Changes That Heal.* Grand Rapids: Zondervan, 1992.

Larry Crabb. *Men and Women: Enjoying the Difference.* Grand Rapids: Zondervan, 1993.

James Dobson. *Straight Talk to Men and Their Wives.* Waco, Tex.: Word, 1980.

James Dobson. *What Wives Wish Their Husbands Knew About Women.* Wheaton, Ill.: Living/Tyndale, 1975.

George Gilder. *Men and Marriage.* Gretna, La.: Pelican, 1986.

Marsha Means. *Living with Your Husband's Secret Wars.* Grand Rapids: Fleming H. Revell/Baker, 1999.

Patrick Means. *Men's Secret Wars.* Grand Rapids: Fleming H. Revell, 1996.

Patrick Morley. *The Man in the Mirror.* Grand Rapids: Zondervan, 1997.

Dennis and Barbara Rainey. *The New Building Your Mate's Self-Esteem*. Nashville: Thomas Nelson, 1995.

Gary Smalley and John Trent. *The Hidden Value of a Man*. Colorado Springs: Focus on the Family, 1992.

Chuck Snyder. *Men: Some Assembly Required*. Colorado Springs: Focus on the Family, 1995.

Chuck and Barb Snyder. *Incompatibility: Still Grounds for a Great Marriage*. Sisters, Ore.: Multnomah, 1999.

Lee and Leslie Strobel. *Surviving a Spiritual Mismatch in Marriage*. Grand Rapids: Zondervan, 2002.

FOUR

Less Fear, Lighter Hearts

❧

*Through many dangers, toils, and snares
I have already come,
'Tis grace that brought me safe thus far,
And grace will lead me home.*

JOHN NEWTON (1725-1807)

*B*eing Christ's disciple while advancing His kingdom within marriage requires the continuous, active application of one's faith in all of life's circumstances, regardless of the surrounding territory. Clearly, our continuing reliance on God's grace, strength, protection, and help isn't a once-and-for-all endeavor. In fact, in any given twenty-four hour period, we shouldn't be surprised to find ourselves lifting up yet another prayer or blessing on behalf of our husband and our marriage for the twentieth time that day!

On some days, it seems possible to accomplish everything God wants of us. On other days, the tasks seem overwhelming. Suddenly, the simple choice of blessing our husband feels very complicated. Where do we find the balance between pleasing God and pleasing others? Who are our life models? What are our responsibilities to our husband? Ourself? The Lord? Where can we even find the *time* to sort out all of these things?

The Generous Grace of God

"What God promises," wrote St. Augustine, "we ourselves do not through choice or nature, but He Himself does by grace."

I have found that it *is* possible to obtain vital answers to these questions when we ask God for direction and discernment regarding our marriage. In the Bible we find this reliable promise: "If any of you lacks wisdom, he should ask God, who gives generously to all without finding fault, and it will be given to him" (James 1:5).

Wherever we are, whatever our age or background, Jesus wants us to know and serve Him. We are His beloved, unique in all creation, with distinctive gifts and talents entrusted to our care for God's great glory. "For we are God's workmanship, created in Christ Jesus to do good works, which God prepared in advance for us to do" (Ephesians 2:10). But notice also these earlier verses: "For it is by grace you have been saved, through faith—and this not from yourselves, it is the gift of God—not by works, so that no one can boast" (Ephesians 2:8-9). Relying on God's grace leads us to more deeply depend on Him as our source of truth and life.

"This is what all the work of grace aims at—an ever deeper knowledge of God, and an ever closer relationship with him," theologian Dr. J. I. Packer tells us. "Grace is God drawing us sinners closer and closer to himself. How does God in grace prosecute this purpose? Not by shielding us from assault by the world, the flesh, and the devil, nor by protecting us from burdensome and frustrating circumstances, nor yet by shielding us from troubles created by our own temperament and psychology; but rather by exposing us to all these things, so as to overwhelm us with a sense of our own inadequacy, and to drive us to cling to him more closely."[1]

When we call on the Lord with a surrendered heart, realizing our complete dependence upon Him, we are drawn into a divine embrace, the mysterious intimacy of a holy relationship with our risen Savior. Waiting upon Him, we grow acutely aware of our need for God.

If we follow Jesus as His disciple and abide in His love, we give Him permission to shape every aspect of our existence. If we live in passionate expectancy of the awesome moment when we reach our life's goal, we allow God to direct our heavenward steps and will find our faith reinforced, our heart protected.

What we think, do, and say has an impact not only on our spirit for eternity, but also upon our heart and mind today. Knowing this, we open ourself for God to fill us with an abiding sense of His plans and purposes for us. Only on the day when we stand before Jesus face-to-face in the glory of His presence will we fully *see* and *understand* our life in light of the one thing that matters: "Not that I have already obtained all this, or have already been made perfect, but I press on to take hold of that for which Christ Jesus took hold of me. Brothers, I do not consider myself yet to have taken hold of it. But one thing I do: Forgetting what is behind and straining toward what is ahead, I press on toward the goal to win the prize for which God has called me in Christ Jesus" (Philippians 3:12-14).

Catching the Little Foxes

As the days go by, married life will continually challenge us to see beyond our own point of view in order to understand where our husband is coming from. How we cope with disappointments, disagreements, and everyday "disasters" directly—and deeply—influences our family relationships. The really big issues of our faith typically aren't as problematic as the accumulated annoyances and strategic satanic attacks, aptly described by Solomon as "the little foxes that are ruining the vineyards" (Song of Solomon 2:15, NASB), which threaten to distract us from our calling as married Christian women.

Wise wives treasure the Holy Spirit's help in discerning and catching the little foxes, revealed in this short list, that nibble and chew away at the fruitful vine of their marriage bond:
- Perfectionism
- Dissatisfaction
- Irresponsibility
- Dependency upon our husband

- Fault-finding
- Poor health habits
- Communication barriers
- Negativity
- Competition
- Sexual coldness
- Inattention to warning signs
- Lack of prayer

Now, let's turn around this summary of damaging attitudes and behaviors. By examining this list of how to avoid each destructive fox, a beautiful picture emerges of what we can do daily to build up our marriage:

- Expect reality; rely on grace
- Be content with your husband; do not compare him to others

❧ ❧ ❧ ———————————————————————————

Press on in Obedience

The power of God is indispensable to altering one's commitment meaningfully. Until I am aware that my needs are already met in Christ, I will be motivated by emptiness to meet my needs. When by simple faith I accept Christ's shed blood as full payment for my sins, I am brought into a relationship with an infinite Being of love and purpose who fully satisfies my deepest needs for security and significance. Therefore I am freed from self-centered preoccupation with my own needs; they are met. It is now possible for me to give to others out of my fullness rather than needing to receive from others because of my emptiness. For the first time, I have the option of living selflessly.

All of us face various character-molding decisions every day. To speak with my spouse, I must consciously and deliberately think: "My purpose right now must be to help my wife realize her value as a person. What can I do that will accomplish this?" My insides may urgently scream with a compelling desire to defend myself, criticize her, or make other manipulative responses. Amid this inner turmoil, I must make a decision to do what will help her feel loved. As I make the choice, the Spirit of God provides the power to make it real—but I must make the choice.

- Accept your responsibility in the marriage
- Replace dependence upon your husband with deeper reliance on Christ
- Forgive your husband's faults
- Care for your health
- Identify communication barriers and tear them down
- Nurture enthusiasm
- Cultivate cooperation
- Foster sexual intimacy
- Pay attention to warning signs; get help when you need it
- Pray and seek wisdom

"By wisdom a house is built, and through understanding it is established; through knowledge its rooms are filled with rare and

---

The natural resistance to truly giving ourselves to the other is rooted in our stubborn fear that if we really give, with no manipulative purpose, we will be shortchanged. Our needs will not be met. At best we'll be disappointed; at worst, we'll be destroyed.

But God is faithful. We are to trust His perfect love to cast out our fear, believing that as we give to our spouses in His name, He will supernaturally bless us with an awareness of His presence. And He will. But it may take time—perhaps months—before we sense His work in us. The willingness to give unconditionally does not come by simply deciding to be selfless. The stain of self-centeredness requires many washings before it no longer controls our motivation. Many commitments to minister and much time spent with God will transpire before we know what it means to give. Our job is to learn faithfulness and to press on in obedience, not giving in to discouragement or weariness, believing that God will always honor the conscious and persevering motivation to serve Him. When a spouse becomes more critical, drinks more heavily, or rejects our ministry, we are to continue in our obedience, believing that our responsibility before God is to obey and trust Him for the outcome.[2]—Larry Crabb

✤ ✤ ✤

beautiful treasures," proclaimed Solomon (Proverbs 24:3-4). Just one glance at this powerful list reveals stunning restoration and beautification possibilities for our marriage, doesn't it? Talk about the ultimate redecorating challenge! And this type of radical redesign, while costly on a personal level, won't break our budget: You can't buy any of the items on this particular list. The gift of our love is at the same time priceless and free.

Since we know that on this side of heaven we will never perfectly love one another, that we will fail time and again as we confront real-life situations with weak flesh, that our broken love will bring us pain as well as pleasure, and that we are covered by God's merciful grace, we can bless our husband with less fear and a lighter heart. May we never forget: We have valuable talents to share with our husband for the glory of our Lord and Savior.

In the strength of God's grace and with His Spirit's help, we can aim to:

- see our husband as the unique creation of our heavenly Father—who loves, accepts, and forgives us by faith in His Son, Jesus Christ;
- give our husband our "accepting presence"—support instead of criticism, practical help instead of simple advice, sacrificial love instead of harsh judgments;
- embrace our husband's God-made manhood as something vitally precious to us—a gift worth blessing, affirming, and celebrating in a world turned upside down by sin; and
- call our husband to greatness, inviting him to become the man God desires him to be as we bless him with the best of our womanly nature—gifts of insight and intuitiveness, tenderness and compassion, and a gentle spirit capable of inwardly reflecting loving activity and calm repose.

So, how and when do we get started? The simplest action becomes a fragrant offering to Jesus when it's performed with love for His glory. We don't have to wait for the perfect moment to surrender ourselves to God and enjoy His partnership in our marital ministry. The time to begin is right now, right where we are, with what we have.

In the next section of this book I'll take a closer look at how we can give our husband these gifts of blessing in specific and practical ways. If you're not already participating in a women's Bible study or other weekly support group for Christian wives where your love for your husband is affirmed and nourished, I recommend you join one. Pray about building a friendship with a mature married woman from whom you can personally receive wise words and mentoring on a regular basis.

As you read, make a note of the blessings and ideas appropriate to your own husband and begin adapting them to your marriage. Start using them all the time, especially when you spot a little fox running through your vineyard.

FOCUS POINTS

- Relying on God's grace leads us to more deeply depend on Him as our source of truth and life.
- If we follow Jesus as His disciple and abide in His love, we give Him permission to shape every aspect of our existence. We allow God to direct our heavenward steps and will find our faith reinforced, our heart protected.
- We are probably less distracted from our calling as Christian wives by the really big issues of faith than by accumulated annoyances and strategic satanic attacks, aptly described by Solomon as "the little foxes that are ruining the vineyards" (Song of Solomon 2:15, NASB).
- The simplest action to trap these foxes becomes a fragrant offering to Jesus when it's performed with love for His glory.

WORDS TO REMEMBER

- Trust in the LORD with all your heart, and do not lean on your own understanding. In all your ways acknowledge him, and he will make straight your paths. (Proverbs 3:5-6, ESV)
- This is what the LORD says—your Redeemer, the Holy One of Israel: "I am the LORD your God, who teaches you what is best for you, who directs you in the way you should go." (Isaiah 48:17)
- I said to the LORD, "You are my Lord; apart from you I have no good thing." (Psalm 16:2)

- Be joyful in hope, patient in affliction, faithful in prayer.
  (Romans 12:12)

REAL GUYS

"WOW, WHAT A WOMAN God has given me! My wife has always loved me for who I am. She is loving and caring and gives me room to grow. She is proud of me and isn't afraid to let the world know. She seems to think, 'Joey knows all things mechanical,' and, 'If you can break it, Joey can fix it,' yet she doesn't volunteer me to do so. There hasn't been a day in our twenty-seven years of marriage that she hasn't told me she loves me. She understands my need to get away on Wednesday nights to go bowling. She prays over my pants (using a hot iron to get the wrinkles out), always doing so with an 'I'd love to, darling.' Have you ever had your pants prayed over? When she is fasting she goes out of her way to make sure I have plenty to eat. She has encouraged me to leave a good job to do what I love, knowing that the move would reduce my stress even though our financial security could greatly suffer. Even though her natural gifting is leadership, she is willing to trust my decision-making even if she thinks there may be another—and it probably is—better way. She understands my need to be the 'man of the house' and she gives me the remote control. (Not that I need the remote or even ask for it; she just understands the why of it.) I'm sure that this just scratches the surface."—Joey

PERSONAL REFLECTIONS

1. What "little foxes" most frequently haunt your marriage vineyard? What steps can you take to begin trapping them and halting their damage?
2. Complete these thoughts in your journal:
   I have felt the joy of blessing my husband most when...
   When I consider Jesus' example of washing His disciples' feet, I feel...
   Honoring and respecting God's gifts as uniquely expressed in my husband's life can best be done by...
3. As you think of all the things you want your marriage to become, what will you do to keep "straining toward the goal" even while you rest in the grace of God?

PRAYERS

Praying God's Blessing for Our Marriage

May my husband and I let the peace of Christ rule in our hearts, since as members of one body we were called to peace. May we always be thankful.—Colossians 3:15

Praying God's Blessing for My Husband

May my husband call upon you, Lord, and may you answer him; may you be with him in trouble, may you deliver him and honor him. May you satisfy my husband with long life and show him your salvation.—Psalm 91:15-16

Closing Prayer

Lord, what is my confidence which I have in this life? Is it not Thou, O Lord, my God, whose mercies are without number? Where hath it ever been well with me without Thee, or where could it be ill with me, when Thou wert present? I rather choose to be a pilgrim on earth with Thee, than without Thee to possess heaven. Where Thou art, there is heaven; and where Thou art not, there is death and hell. There is none that can help me in my necessities, but only Thou, my God; Thou art my Hope, Thou my Confidence. Although Thou exposest me to diverse temptations and adversities, yet Thou orderest all this to my advantage; in which trial of me Thou oughtest no less to be loved and praised than if Thou didst fill me full of heavenly consolations. Amen.[3]—Thomas à Kempis (1380-1471)

BLESSINGS NOW

- Seek God's wisdom for your marriage. Ask God to give you insight and direction as you discern and catch any of these "little foxes" that may be disrupting your relationship: perfectionism, dissatisfaction, irresponsibility, dependency upon your husband, fault-finding, poor health habits, communication barriers, negativity, competition, sexual coldness, inattention to warning signs, and lack of prayer.
- Encourage your husband's interests. Accompany him on an excursion of his choosing. Enjoy the ride!
- Call upon God with a surrendered heart, realizing your complete dependence upon Him. As you wait upon the Lord,

be attentive of your constant need for His strength and
sustenance.

- Depend upon the unchanging truth of God's Word and the
active guidance of His Holy Spirit rather than on what your
current day-to-day life experiences and emotions "say" to you
about love and marriage. Using index cards or self-stick notes,
copy several verses that seem particularly relevant to you today
and refer to them often.

- Compliment your husband in public, as well as in private. Let
him know you approve of him not only for what he has done,
but also for who he is.

- Using one of the following questions, spend some time listening to your husband and giving him your focused attention. If
it turns out that he's had a hard day and/or is not feeling especially communicative, be gracious. Respond with supportive
understanding:

  ◊ How are you feeling tonight?
  ◊ What was the best thing about this day for you?
  ◊ Did you learn anything new at work?
  ◊ How did you feel when that happened today?
  ◊ Feel like sharing what's on your mind with me?
  ◊ What were some of the highlights of your day?

- View your mate as the unique creation of God that he is, often
remembering he is "God's workmanship, created in Christ
Jesus to do good works, which God prepared in advance for
[him] to do" (Ephesians 2:10).

- Anticipate your husband's needs. Take a risk by doing something surprising and daring rather than being overly practical.

- Make reservations for an overnight stay together at an elegant
resort or hotel. Pack lightly.

- Spend ample time privately praying for your husband early in
the morning, talking freely with God about your husband's
needs and hopes and frustrations. Ask the Lord to prompt you
to pray for your beloved at specific times in specific ways
throughout the day.

FOR FURTHER READING

Henry T. Blackaby and Claude V. King. *Experiencing God: Knowing and Doing His Will.* Nashville: Lifeway, 1994.

Bryan Chapell. *Each for the Other: Marriage As It's Meant to Be.* Grand Rapids: Baker, 1998.

Henry Cloud and John Townsend. *Boundaries in Marriage.* Grand Rapids: Zondervan, 1999.

Sharon A. Hersh. *Bravehearts: Unlocking the Courage to Love with Abandon.* Colorado Springs: WaterBrook, 2000.

Jerry Jenkins. *Loving Your Marriage Enough to Protect It.* Chicago: Moody, 1993.

Peter Kreeft. *Back to Virtue.* San Francisco: Ignatius, 1992.

Robert Boyd Munger. *My Heart—Christ's Home.* Downers Grove, Ill.: InterVarsity, 1992.

John and Teri Nieder. *The Marriage Maker: The Holy Spirit and the Hidden Power of Becoming One.* Eugene, Ore.: Harvest House, 1996.

Dennis Rainey. *We Still Do.* Nashville: Thomas Nelson, 2001.

Edith Schaeffer. *What Is a Family?* Old Tappan, N.J.: Fleming H. Revell, 1975.

Gary Smalley and John Trent. *Love Is a Decision: Proven Techniques to Keep Your Marriage Alive and Healthy.* Nashville: Word, 1989.

Hannah Whitall Smith. *The Christian's Secret of a Happy Life.* Westwood, N.J.: Spire/Fleming H. Revell, 1970.

Corrie ten Boom. *Not I, but Christ.* Grand Rapids: Fleming H. Revell, 1997.

John White. *The Fight: A Practical Handbook for Christian Living.* Downer's Grove, Ill.: InterVarsity, 1976.

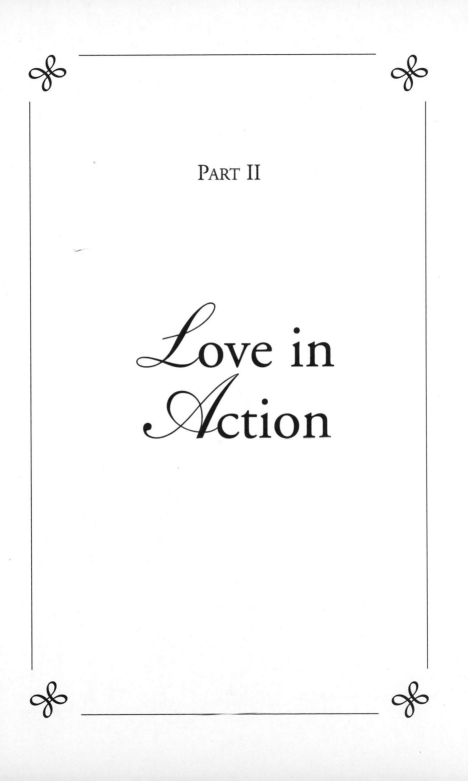

PART II

Love in Action

FIVE

The Blessings of Right Priorities

When the cares of my heart are many,
your consolations cheer my soul.
PSALM 94:19, ESV

*I*t promised to be just another wild day, filled with phone calls and appointments and settling assorted sibling disputes, not to mention doing four loads of laundry, paying a month's worth of bills, fixing dinner, and hosting a small group Bible study. By two in the afternoon I was experiencing a bona fide adrenaline high; by seven, the only welcome I could muster in response to our guests' arrival was a meager grin and a turn of my hand that suggested, "Let's sit down, shall we?" Smiling but nervous, I hoped to convey a certain degree of calmness when in fact I felt like collapsing. In a warm bath. With the door locked. For the rest of the evening.

Ninety uneventful minutes passed, after which the children had to be picked up from youth activities at church, bedtime rituals supervised, dishes done, and more phone calls made—a fairly typical pattern at our home on Wednesday nights during those years. But this particular evening, just as I prepared to go sink into the depths of my tub, David suggested we go out for a walk. Alone. Right away.

Incredulous at first, I realized my husband was serious and probably wanted to talk. So I popped on my shoes, threw on a sweater, and
followed him out the front door.

We were greeted by wisps of wind and a sparkling sky scattered
with stars, which immediately drew our attention upward. *So this is
what You wanted to show me, Lord,* I thought, *a view of things from a
larger perspective...*

As I listened to David, the stillness of the night and the repetitive
motion of our steps settled my frazzled nerves. Over the course of three
miles, my muscles worked out their tension. It was enough just to *be
there* in that moment, walking under the stars with my husband, quietly
communing with the Lord each in our own way, knowing we weren't
alone in the universe, sensing God's merciful love accompanying us.

Such moments seem to arrive from out of the blue—hand-delivered
from our all-knowing Father—as unexpected reminders of His personal attentiveness, and I am always thankful for His timely intervention. Yet, somehow, I am still delightfully surprised when the Holy
Spirit touches my heart and my marriage in this way, with peace and
joy and wonder, in the midst of my toil and tiredness.

How many opportunities for blessing and celebration have I
missed with my husband because of my determined choice to stick to
a schedule or remain preoccupied with my daily work? I don't even
want to know. I'm sure the answer would reveal a too-often-repeated
scenario of heartache and disappointment resulting from time spent
ignoring my Savior's all-too-obvious cues. Yet Jesus continues to comfort and strengthen me. With unmistakable clarity His Word sends its
incredible message:

YOU ARE LOVED.

Torn-to-Pieces-Hood

"Whoever gets sense loves his own soul," observed Solomon (Proverbs
19:8, ESV). "Getting sense" requires knowledge and self-control as we
balance our need for activity and rest, intimacy and privacy, speaking
and listening, caring for our husband and caring for ourself, spending
time with others and spending time alone with the Lord. Finding and

maintaining this ever-elusive balance is an ongoing challenge; neglecting or denying our need for this balance can turn even fruitful lives
into bone-dry wastelands.

Anne Morrow Lindbergh wonderfully expressed our uniquely
feminine need for balance in the midst of marital and family activities—and the life-giving benefits we reap if we heed this need—when
she wrote:

> I would like to achieve a state of inner spiritual grace from
> which I could function and give as I was meant to in the eye of
> God.... This is an end toward which we should strive—to be
> the still axis within the revolving wheel of relationships, obliga-
> tions, and activities. Solitude alone is not the answer to this; it
> is only a step toward it, a mechanical aid.... The problem is
> more how to still the soul in the midst of activities. In fact, the
> problem is how to feed the soul.
>
> For it is the spirit of woman that is going dry, not the mechan-
> ics that are wanting.... With our garnered free time, we are more
> apt to drain our creative springs than to refill them. With our
> pitchers, we attempt sometimes to water a field, not a garden.
>
> Not knowing how to feed the spirit, we try to muffle its
> demands and distractions. Instead of stilling the center, the axis
> of the wheel, we add more centrifugal activities to our lives—
> which tend to throw us off balance.
>
> [The] answer is not in the frequent pursuit of centrifugal
> activities which only lead in the end to fragmentation. Woman's
> life today is tending more and more toward the state
> [described] so well in the German word, "Zerrissenheit—torn-
> to-pieces-hood." She cannot live perpetually in "Zerrissenheit."
> She will be shattered into a thousand pieces. On the contrary,
> she must consciously encourage those pursuits which oppose
> the centrifugal forces of today.[1]

Do you, like Anne Morrow Lindbergh, long to "achieve a state of
inner spiritual grace" from which you can function with womanly
wholeness?

We know following Jesus in the midst of life as it actually is comprises the greatest challenge—and highest privilege—of our days. We believe true discipleship requires strong, steadfast faith and a daily commitment to choose the right path. We understand that yielding to the power of God's grace and the direction of the Holy Spirit is neither comfortable nor automatic. Still, it's easy for us to get distracted.

Living perpetually in "torn-to-pieces-hood" just doesn't make sense, nor does it fit the new way of life God calls us to enjoy, as it is so beautifully described here by the apostle Paul: "Present your bodies as a living sacrifice, holy and acceptable to God, which is your spiritual worship. Do not be conformed to this world, but be transformed by the renewal of your mind, that by testing you may discern what is the will of God, what is good and acceptable and perfect" (Romans 12:1-2, ESV).

To whom does our heart belong? Upon whom do we most deeply depend for our identity, value, and security? If our hearts belong to Christ and we firmly rely upon Him to direct our thoughts, deeds, and actions, how will this affect our wifely roles and responsibilities—and our ability to bless our husband?

❧ ❧ ❧ ⎯⎯⎯⎯⎯⎯⎯⎯⎯⎯⎯⎯⎯⎯⎯⎯⎯⎯⎯⎯⎯⎯⎯⎯

The Art of Flexibility

Most women would like to have their days scheduled from beginning to end, with no surprises. Schedules can be beneficial when they provide a guide for the day, but they can also become inflexible taskmasters. The day is ruined for some women when one item on their schedule has to be changed. All they can think when their husbands come home is, "I'm behind on my schedule, and tomorrow will be worse if I don't catch up before bedtime."

If you want your marital relationship to deepen, it is very important that you learn to be flexible. I believe there is nothing as important to you or your family as a good, loving relationship with your husband. Your flexibility can

For the sake of our heart *and* our husband, we need to turn to the Lord to replenish our inner springs when we start running dry.

Only One Thing Is Essential

The familiar New Testament story of Mary and Martha contains a valuable lesson for those of us who feel weighed down by life's demands:

> As Jesus and his disciples were on their way, he came to a village where a woman named Martha opened her home to him. She had a sister called Mary, who sat at the Lord's feet listening to what he said. But Martha was distracted by all the preparations that had to be made. She came to him and asked, "Lord, don't you care that my sister has left me to do the work by myself? Tell her to help me!"
>
> "Martha, Martha," the Lord answered, "you are worried and upset about many things, but only one thing is needed. Mary has chosen what is better, and it will not be taken away from her." (Luke 10:38-42)

---

make your husband feel really special and keep that "spark" in your relationship. When he comes home and sees that you are willing to set aside your schedule for an unrushed conversation, he feels valued and loved.

Occasionally I come home late at night after meeting with a couple or a group. It really means a lot to me when my wife wakes up and spends a few minutes listening to me unwind as I tell her about my evening. Sure she's making a sacrifice, but it makes me feel important and deepens my affection for her.

Your schedule is important, I realize. However, you need to maintain a balance by being able to set aside your priorities from time to time to pay special attention to your husband and his needs. That's genuine love.[2]
—Gary Smalley

Have you, like Martha, sometimes found yourself asking, "Lord, don't you care?" Do your personal priorities threaten to take precedence over what is better? When it's clear that your husband has left you to do all the work by yourself—leaving you feeling shut out or left behind—how do you respond?

Our natural inclination when we're under pressure is to compete, to compare, to blame, to criticize, to demand, or to interrupt—and our husband often finds himself directly in the line of fire. Martha, no doubt, was wholeheartedly going about her business when she reached her stress limit. But Jesus didn't offer her His sympathy. Instead, He offered a gentle rebuke.

Like Martha, our hearts are distracted and weighed down by many worthwhile things—concerns about family and friends, daily work responsibilities, church-related duties, financial needs—as well as by our own ongoing thoughts, judgments, and self-talk. Looking to our Lord's peace and inviting His love to reign in our hearts relieves hurt, eases weariness, and sets our feet back on solid ground. This is not an easy task by any means; when fatigue sets in, harsh words erect barriers and marital tension mounts. But given the alternative, what kind of life together would you truly prefer?

Paul proclaimed: "My purpose is that they may be encouraged in heart and united in love, so that they may have the full riches of complete understanding, in order that they may know the mystery of God, namely, Christ, in whom are hidden all the treasures of wisdom and knowledge" (Colossians 2:2-3). Yielding our heart and mind to the Holy Spirit's direction transforms our whole outlook. The more we pay attention to our Shepherd's gentle reproof and trustworthy guidance, the less we find ourself worrying about the things that don't matter.

"Choose—day after day," Edith Schaeffer encourages us. "Choose to sit in the dark and wait for His guidance. Choose to sit at His feet and accept the completeness of His truth. Choose as Mary did in Luke 10, as she sat at Jesus' feet and concentrated on what He was teaching. It was not that Jesus was saying that housework was unnecessary—He himself cooked fish for the disciples—but that there was at that time a choice to be made.... Day by day and moment by moment, choose carefully whom you will listen to and whom you will serve."[3]

Choosing to wait upon the Lord—to surrender our anxieties about the cares of each day to Him as we draw fresh strength from His indwelling Spirit—requires recognizing the one thing Jesus said is needed: "But seek first his kingdom and his righteousness" (Matthew 6:33). By continually seeking God's help "in the Spirit on all occasions with all kinds of prayers and requests" (Ephesians 6:18), our heart finds rest. Concentrating our heart on the Word of God makes us wise and keeps us focused. "The wise woman builds her house…. Wisdom reposes in the heart of the discerning," noted King Solomon, adding, "The tongue of the wise commends knowledge" (Proverbs 14:1, 33; 15:2).

Taking the time to slow down long enough to talk to God and delight in the joy of His sweet presence—wherever we are, regardless of what we are doing, whether it's doing the dishes or driving to the store or shuttling the school car pool or preparing for an important meeting—can quiet our heart and mind like nothing else. This is where we find the hidden strength that can never be taken away from us.

FOCUS POINTS

- If we pay attention, God will surprise us with hand-delivered moments that touch our heart and marriage with peace and joy and wonder in the midst of our toil and tiredness. He wants to remind us of His attentiveness, of His great love for us.
- Living perpetually in "torn-to-pieces-hood" just doesn't make sense, nor does it fit the new way of life God calls us to enjoy. For the sake of our heart *and* our husband, we need to turn to the Lord to replenish our inner springs when we start running dry.
- In the busyness of life, choose to wait on the Lord, waiting in prayer and in His Word. Looking to His peace and inviting His love to reign in our heart relieves hurt, eases weariness, and sets our feet back on solid ground.

WORDS TO REMEMBER

- O God, you are my God, earnestly I seek you; my soul thirsts for you, my body longs for you, in a dry and weary land where there is no water. I have seen you in the sanctuary and beheld your power and your glory. (Psalm 63:1-2)

• Wait for the LORD; be strong and take heart and wait for the LORD. (Psalm 27:14)

• My soul finds rest in God alone; my salvation comes from him. He alone is my rock and my salvation; he is my fortress, I will never be shaken. (Psalm 62:1-2)

• Fret not thyself. (Psalm 37:1, KJV)

• Do not be anxious about anything, but in everything, by prayer and petition, with thanksgiving, present your requests to God. And the peace of God, which transcends all understanding, will guard your hearts and your minds in Christ Jesus. (Philippians 4:6-7)

REAL GUYS

"My wife is very affirming in everything she says about me, whether or not I am present. We teach a course on Marriage Enrichment together, and her gracious comments always encourage me. Her gifts involve serving behind the scene to make everything—our marriage of thirty years, our family, and our ministry together—run smoothly and seamlessly. She laughs at my humor, even when she knows the punch line, and has a way of smiling that communicates our love still burns brightly. Through many trials and difficulties (medical and financial) she has been absolutely unwavering in her commitment to God and to me."—Bill

PERSONAL REFLECTIONS

1. The following passage, written by the brilliant Carmelite nun Teresa of Avila, is printed on a bookmark I use every day in my Bible. Teresa's words have often reminded me to slow down and think of the bigger picture when I'm facing a stressful day. What do her words say to you today?

   Let nothing disturb you.
   Let nothing terrify you.
   All things pass away.

God is unchangeable.
Patience gains everything.
He who clings to God wants nothing.
God alone is sufficient.—Teresa of Avila (1515-1582)

2. Complete the following thoughts in your journal:

*When I start to live "out of balance," the area of my life that
suffers most is usually...*

*For me, the greatest obstacle to refilling my inner springs
creatively lies in my choice to...*

*When Jesus told Martha, "Mary has chosen what is better,"
I think He might have meant...*

3. Recall a time when God surprised you by "showing up" with
His grace and peace in the middle of a busy day. What
prompted you to notice? What might have happened if you
had missed it? How did the moment change you?

PRAYERS

Praying God's Blessing for Our Marriage

Heavenly Father, send forth your light and your truth, let them
guide us; let them bring us to your holy mountain, to the place where
you dwell. (Psalm 43:3)

Praying God's Blessing for My Husband

May my husband accept your words, Lord, and store up your
commands in his heart, turning his ear to wisdom and applying his
heart to understanding. (Proverbs 2:1-2)

Closing Prayer

O Thou full of compassion, I commit and commend myself unto
Thee, in whom I am, and live, and know. Be Thou the Goal of my
pilgrimage, and my Rest by the way. Let my soul take refuge from the
crowding turmoil of worldly thoughts beneath the shadow of Thy
wings; let my heart, this sea of restless waves, find peace in Thee, O
God. Thou bounteous Giver of all good gifts, give to her who is weary
refreshing food; gather our distracted thoughts and powers into harmony again; and set the prisoner free. See, she stands at Thy door and
knocks; be it opened up to her, that she may enter with a free step, and

be quickened by Thee. For Thou art the Well-spring of Life, the Light of eternal Brightness, wherein the just live who love Thee. Be it unto me according to Thy word. Amen.[4]—Augustine of Hippo (354-430)

Blessings Now

- Take your everyday life and place it before God as an offering first thing each morning.

- Pursue peace and contentment: Turn to the Lord to replenish your inner springs when you start running dry. Reflect on Psalm 23, gathering strength from its reassuring promises: "The LORD is my shepherd, I shall not be in want. He makes me lie down in green pastures, he leads me beside quiet waters, he restores my soul. He guides me in paths of righteousness for his name's sake" (Psalm 23:1-3).

- Hug your husband and ask him how he feels today. Note the tone of his voice and his body language. After hearing his reply and deciphering the unspoken messages he sends you, show him your loving care and concern.

- Relieve your hurt, ease your weariness, and set your feet back on solid ground by looking to the Lord and again inviting His love to reign in your heart. Remember, you are:
    ◊ a precious child of your heavenly Father (Matthew 7:11).
    ◊ a co-heir with Christ (Romans 8:17).
    ◊ a person granted the protection of angels (Psalm 91:11).
    ◊ a servant of God, not the world's slave (Romans 6:22).
    ◊ a temple of the living God (2 Corinthians 6:16).
    ◊ a redeemed, justified, cleansed, protected, forgiven, blessed, highly valued, and eternally loved woman!

- Choose to wait upon the Lord—to surrender your anxieties about today to Him as you draw fresh strength from His indwelling Spirit—by recognizing the one thing Jesus said is needed: "Seek first his kingdom and his righteousness" (Matthew 6:33).

- Quiet your heart and mind. Take the time to slow down long enough to talk to God and delight in the joy of His sweet presence—wherever you happen to be, regardless of what you are doing.

- When fatigue sets in, don't be surprised when harsh words erect barriers and marital tension mounts. Stop, take a break, get some rest. Refuse to join the destructive dance of disappointment and anger that weakens, rather than reinforces, your marriage bond.
- Challenge some of the unnecessary "oughts" and "shoulds" that currently pile pressure and stress on your marriage relationship. Are you facing any self-imposed deadlines that can be eliminated or postponed? Reduce unwelcome sources of tension to whatever extent you can.
- Schedule a silent retreat for spiritual renewal, alone or together. Dedicate this time to refilling your inner springs and stilling your soul before God.
- Love your husband actively even when you think you have a valid reason not to tenderly respond or care. Go to a solitary place and spend some time alone with God in prayer, asking the Lord's love for your husband to revive your own. Depend on Jesus to quietly express His love through you.

FOR FURTHER READING

Sister Wendy Beckett. *Meditations on Joy*. London: Dorling Kindersley, 1995.

Esther Burroughs. *Splash the Living Water: Turning Daily Interruptions into Life-Giving Encounters*. Nashville: Thomas Nelson, 1999.

Larry Crabb. *Inside Out*. Colorado Springs: NavPress, 1988.

Jean-Pierre de Caussade. *The Sacrament of the Present Moment*. Kitty Muggeridge, trans. San Francisco: Harper & Row, 1982.

Jean Fleming. *Feeding Your Soul: A Quiet Time Handbook*. Colorado Springs: NavPress, 1999.

Richard J. Foster. *Freedom of Simplicity*. San Francisco: Harper & Row, 1981.

Cynthia Heald. *Becoming a Woman of Freedom*. Colorado Springs: NavPress, 1992.

Jan Johnson. *Enjoying the Presence of God*. Colorado Springs: NavPress, 1996.

Anne Morrow Lindbergh. *Gift from the Sea*. New York: Pantheon, 1955.

Catherine Marshall. *Beyond Our Selves*. Grand Rapids: Chosen/Baker, 2001.

Roger McGee. *The Search for Significance*. Houston: Rapha, 1990.

David Seamands. *Healing Grace: Letting God Free You from the Performance Trap*. Wheaton, Ill.: Victor, 1988.

Luci Shaw. *Water My Soul*. Grand Rapids: Zondervan, 1998.

Joni Eareckson Tada. *A Quiet Place in a Crazy World*. Portland, Ore.: Multnomah, 1993.

Gigi Graham Tchividjian. *For Women Only: Keeping Your Balance in a Changing World*. Grand Rapids: Baker, 2001.

Corrie ten Boom. *Each New Day*. Minneapolis: World Wide, 1977.

A. W. Tozer. *The Pursuit of God*. Camp Hill, Penn.: Christian Publications, 1982.

Ingrid Trobisch. *The Confident Woman: Finding Quiet Strength in a Turbulent World*. San Francisco: HarperSanFrancisco, 1993.

Ramona Cramer Tucker. *The Busy Woman's Guide to a Balanced Life*. Wheaton, Ill.: Tyndale, 1997.

SIX

The Blessings of Self-Care and Spiritual Growth

❧

The more I succeed in accepting myself
as a physical creature, the more I am able
to live in harmony and peace with myself.
INGRID TROBISCH

*J*esus seemed to understand the importance of setting aside time to be alone with His Father, away from the demands of ministry to the multitudes. You, too, need a time of peace and quiet on a daily basis, consciously removing yourself from that disastrous state of *zer-rissenheit*. In addition, you need basic nutrients, exercise, sleep, and the appropriate expression of your emotions. By recognizing and respecting how your body functions, you will discover a new appreciation for what it is, and isn't, capable of. Through accepting your limitations as well as your abilities, you can adopt a lifestyle that fits your physical, emotional, and spiritual needs. Heeding the admonition "Take care of yourself" can pay multiple personal and marital dividends. It's just good, plain common sense to pay attention to what your body "tells" you, and then wisely meet your requirements with a variety of healthful foods, adequate rest, and refreshing recreation. After meeting these important needs, other activities can take place with greater ease.

What Does This Have to Do with My Husband?

Do you know what it's like to feel so spent that you find yourself dreaming of solitary, behind-locked-doors escapes instead of time alone with your husband? I imagine you do.

God has given us women minds and bodies that are remarkably sensitive to the ebb and flow of life; our Maker has created us to be wonderfully different from men. The frazzled existence many of us lead demands persistent reevaluation. When our real hunger for rest and refreshment is filled through our private fellowship with God, we usually find we have much more to give to our husband.

One aspect of lovingly blessing and supporting each other in marriage is to share one another's burdens while at the same time doing what we can to carry our own. This kind of partnership can significantly decrease the stressful aspects of our life while promoting our spiritual growth. God's Word tells us: "Carry each other's burdens, and in this way you will fulfill the law of Christ." It also says, "Each one should test his own actions. Then he can take pride in himself, without comparing himself to somebody else, for each one should carry his own load" (Galatians 6:2, 4-5). Of course, carrying our own responsibilities can be difficult enough when we're physically and spiritually depleted.

"One reason why Christian women have such a hard time accepting themselves, including their bodies, is because the idea still prevails that the spiritual and mental areas of our lives are somehow closer to God, more pleasing to him and more 'Christian' than the physical realm," observes author and educator Ingrid Trobisch. "The Bible, which calls the body the 'temple of the Holy Spirit,' says the contrary: the more authentic our faith is, the more we are able to live at peace with our bodies."[1]

Inwardly responding to the changing currents of our daily life according to our womanly nature requires wisdom. It makes no sense to discount the kind of self-care that distinctly blesses our husband. Our spiritual, emotional, and physical health is protected and promoted when we honor God's design for our heart, soul, mind, and body, resulting in blessings not only for us, but also for the man we married.

Understanding the rhythms and reactions of your mind and body makes sense and can also help your husband better understand you. Doing what you can to take care of yourself and alleviate the more challenging aspects of your cyclical nature is an ongoing responsibility. The good news is that even when your ability to cope is thwarted, when your stress level mounts beyond your tolerance limit, your faith can thrive in the absence of emotional or physical strength.

"We Understand"

It was an early morning in late summer, and we were in the midst of a record-breaking heat wave. Temperatures had hovered in the three-digit range for more than a week. Our air conditioner had broken down a few days before, so each day the tension level in our home rose right along with the thermometer, Popsicles and Kool-Aid notwithstanding.

As I got dressed to go to the dentist, I noticed how relatively cool and calm the air was. The kids were still in bed, a soft breeze was blowing through the windows, and my stress hormones had taken the night off. Even the prospect of sitting in the dentist's chair for ninety minutes sounded fairly relaxing. But a strange thing happened to me on my way to the dentist's office: Just when I thought I had it all together, I suddenly burst into tears. A river of them.

In the ten-block distance between my front door and Dr. Larson's building, I managed to soak my last two Kleenex and rinse off all my mascara. Worse yet, I wasn't sure I would be able to *stop* crying once I got inside the office. Swallowing my pride, I blew my nose on a well-used tissue, blotted the black smudges under my eyes, and headed in for my appointment.

After a brief (and tearless) pause in Dr. Larson's waiting room, her dental assistant escorted me to the familiar chair. As soon as I sat down, however, my eyes welled up again. Not knowing what else to say, I told the assistant I was feeling "more emotional" than usual and warned her I might need several tissues. With genuine compassion, she promptly put an entire box of Kleenex in my lap. Adjusting the headphones, I turned to the classical channel, lay back in the recliner, took a deep cleansing breath, and hoped I could stave off the sniffles for the next hour and a half. I wondered how in the world I would wipe my eyes with the safety goggles on my head. In the meantime, Dr. Larson came in, said a brief hello, and began the treatment.

Then, one by one, the tears began to trickle down under the rim of my goggles onto my cheeks. Dr. Larson's assistant alternately dabbed and suctioned, never missing a beat.

"Is this your time of the month?" she asked.

Unable to answer, I nodded affirmatively.

"We both know how *that* is," chimed in Dr. Larson, who was in her fourth month of pregnancy. She went on to explain that earlier in the week, on her day off, she had spent the entire afternoon blubbering in the bathtub. Blinking back the tears, I looked up at her with appreciative amazement. "We understand," she said, looking right back. "Feel free to just go ahead and cry. After you leave here today,

❧ ❧ ❧ ───────────────────────────────

Live with It, Not Against It!

A husband once asked me, "Why is my wife never the same two days in a row?" If he had taken the trouble to understand what happens to his wife in her body during the monthly cycle, he would know the answer. . . .

To accept yourself as a woman means to live consciously with your cycle: live with it and not against it! Therefore, self-awareness is an essential part of self-acceptance. This is just as essential for the single woman as for the married woman. The woman who is aware of her cycle is able to anticipate and then prepare. To know what causes difficulties reduces fear.

Even the daily schedule can be adjusted to the cycle to a certain degree. With a little bit of planning, one can avoid doing spring cleaning, having a

my prescription for you is *please, take good care of yourself.* Dentist's orders."

What a relief! I was so thankful to be in the presence of tenderhearted professionals at that moment. Although I can laugh about it now, the gentle empathy extended to me by those two women—who asked for neither explanation nor apology—was truly comforting on that humid August morning.

This Never-Ending Process

We understand. Only a woman can understand what it's like to live with the predictable unpredictability of a cyclical nature, no offense to our dear husband, of course. Only a woman can describe what it's like on certain days when she is more sensitive to stress, tense times that tend to accompany ovulation and menstruation, pregnancy, perimenopause, and postmenopause. Reactions vary from mild irritability to near-suicidal despair and are *real.* (Few women know how to sob on cue.)

Without looking at a calendar, most women know when they're about to begin menstruating. Breast tenderness, water retention, abdominal discomfort, altered blood sugar metabolism, and a wide

---

large dinner party, or even moving just during the days of premenstrual tension. A husband who helps his wife to plan helps her at the same time to live in harmony with her cycle.

But this is only possible if he knows where she stands. Then he can understand also why she may be sad without reason, or irritated without an apparent cause. He knows that this is not a fault of her character as his wife, but can simply be steered by her hormones. Thus he can see it all in the right perspective, which will help him to respond in the right way and not with biting irony. "That's just the way a woman is—incalculable and illogical." It's the time for kind humor, a comforting word, or a good and understanding silence.[2]—Ingrid Trobisch

❀ ❀ ❀

variety of significant stress-related symptoms are experienced by nearly 75 percent of menstrual women. For others, premenstrual symptoms are more severe. During pregnancy and lactation, other similar physical and emotional changes appear. After menopause or the surgical removal of the ovaries, continuing hormonal ups and downs are not unusual. Learning to live wisely with one's body, it seems, was divinely designed to be a continuous process. Sharing our hard-won insights with our husband requires creative communication and an ample amount of humor—after the tears stop flowing, that is.

Coping with the ups and downs of the menstrual cycle—or the absence of it—can be a challenge, to say the least. Vitamin supplements, hormonal preparations, herbal remedies, prescribed medications, and/or special dietary regimens can be used with success to reduce the severity of associated symptoms. Stress management techniques, when wisely and effectively employed, also help many women significantly relieve hormonally related tension. Constructive self-talk and other cognitive coping strategies can be useful relief measures as well.

Yet hormonal levels fluctuate through each phase of a woman's life; no single relief measure can cancel our ongoing need for the hormones unique to our gender. These chemical messengers trigger activity in thousands of cells month after month, year after year, intricately orchestrating a harmony between our mind and body that at times seems to slip out of tune. While self-help strategies may serve to reduce the discord, none can silence it entirely.

Strength in Our Weakness

Have you found that coping with your body's predictable unpredictability has become problematic for your marriage? Have you—or your husband—ever wished you were a little *less* complex?

At face value, being a woman is, at least in a biological sense, considerably more complicated and challenging than being a man. But over the years I have discovered there is a fascinating advantage in my complexity: When I am at my weakest, I can trust the Lord to be strong. What some might associate with weakness has become one of the things that make me most resilient, more open to what God can do. Moments of discomforting physical and emotional vulnerability often have brought my faith a genuine expectancy; increased sensitivity to surrounding circumstances, even on difficult days, has repeatedly led me into intimate fellowship with God. When combined with appropriate self-care, this not-always-comfortable aspect of my nature has often been not only a blessing for me, but also for my husband. The spiritual growth prompted by my regularly recurring peaks and valleys benefits both David and me, though at the time we may be loath to admit it. Typically, it's only in retrospect, long after a difficult bout with some cyclically induced hormonal event, that I look back and see how these uniquely feminine lessons touched our marriage in some positive way.

As I sat in the dentist's chair weeping that summer morning, this truth hit home in a new way: Though I was swept up in a flash flood of emotion complicated by stress, fatigue, hundred-degree temperatures, hormones, financial concerns, four active children, and a discouraged husband, I realized that no matter how overwhelmed I *felt*, God's promises remained firm.

"It is sometimes thought that the emotions are the governing power of our nature," notes Hannah Whitall Smith. "But I think all of us know, as a matter of practical experience, that there is something within us, behind our emotions and our wishes, an independent self, that, after all, decides everything and controls everything. Our emotions belong to us, and are suffered and enjoyed by us, but they are not ourselves; and if God is to take possession of us, it must be into this central will or personality that He enters."[3]

This is it! The key to unlocking the secret of knowing God's strength in the midst of our weaknesses is choosing to reach out to our Savior for help and direction when we are tempted to cling to our concerns instead. It is not in denying who we are, the amount of stress we're under, or how we feel, but doing what we can to become healthy while believing the Lord is present, available, and interested in every aspect of our being. (See Appendix 6.1, "To Your Health," and Appendix 6.2, "Calm, Cool, and Collected.")

Please, take good care of yourself. Each of us has a limit to the amount of stress we can cope with before our body and mind react, and some of us can't handle as much stress as the next person. We are not all created equal when it comes to our ability to withstand life's daily demands. Assessing our personal priorities; identifying what produces the greatest time, energy, and financial pressures in us; developing a plan that helps alleviate these pressures; and promoting our health will lighten our stress load.

"From the ends of the earth I call to you, I call as my heart grows faint; lead me to the rock that is higher than I. For you have been my refuge, a strong tower against the foe" (Psalm 61:2-3). Although self-help solutions and professional diagnoses contribute to our overall health, nothing can substitute for seeking our Rock of refuge in a time of need. Having done all we can in effectively using the medical and alternative relief measures available to us, we can seek the hidden strength and serenity God alone can give.

FOCUS POINTS

- Each of us needs a unique combination of basic nutrients, exercise, sleep, recreation, and the space to appropriately express our emotions. We also need a time of peace and quiet on a daily basis, consciously removing ourselves from that disastrous state of *zerrissenheit*.
- By respecting our body, we will discover a new appreciation for what we are—and aren't—capable of. Through accepting our limitations as well as our abilities, we can adopt a lifestyle that fits our physical, emotional, and spiritual needs. After meeting these important needs, other activities—including caring for our husband and family—can take place with greater ease.
- The more frustrating symptoms of a woman's physiology can be relieved, but never entirely eliminated. Yet no matter how we feel, God's promises stand firm. In our weakness, He makes us strong, because He is deeply concerned with our whole being.

WORDS TO REMEMBER

- I lift up my eyes to the hills—where does my help come from? My help comes from the LORD, the Maker of heaven and earth. (Psalm 121:1-2)

- Do you not know that your body is a temple of the Holy Spirit, who is in you, whom you have received from God? You are not your own; you were bought at a price. Therefore honor God with your body. (1 Corinthians 6:19-20)
- If anyone acknowledges that Jesus is the Son of God, God lives in him and he in God. (1 John 4:15)
- Heal me, O LORD, and I will be healed; save me and I will be saved, for You are my praise. (Jeremiah 17:14, NASB)
- I have been crucified with Christ and I no longer live, but Christ lives in me. The life I live in the body, I live by faith in the Son of God, who loved me and gave himself for me. (Galatians 2:20)

REAL GUYS

"One of our first missionary assignments after Janna and I married took us to Holland, where we were treated to 'mosselsoep,' a customary soup of Janna's least favorite flavor: mussels. I felt terrible and started to explain that Janna wasn't able to eat it, but she didn't even bat an eye. She ate her entire serving, and all I could think was, *This woman loves me.* Afterward, she thanked our hosts with another of their customs: a big, deep belch."—Frank

PERSONAL REFLECTIONS

1. Of your physical needs (such as rest, fitness, nutrition, healing), which most needs your attention right now? What steps can you take toward meeting that need? Set a goal and ask your husband or a close friend to encourage you in your efforts.
2. Complete the following thoughts in your journal:
   When I fail to take care of myself, it is usually because...
   When I've been spending time alone with the Lord, I notice a real difference in...
   When I feel well physically, I can do a better job of...
3. There is a direct correlation between our overall health and our ability to successfully order and attend to our priorities (see chapter 5). How might taking care of yourself alleviate

the stress you feel as the result of *not* accomplishing your priorities? What do you believe God is asking you to do as you seek the best way to order your life in service to Him and others?

PRAYERS

Praying God's Blessing for Our Marriage

May we find our strength in you, Lord; strengthen us in your mighty power.—Ephesians 6:10

Praying God's Blessing for My Husband

Lord, thank you for being with my husband; I know you are mighty to save. May you take great delight in my husband, and quiet him with your love; may you rejoice over him with singing.—Zephaniah 3:17

Closing Prayer

O Thou who has created all things, O Thou who knowest all things, O Father who seest all our weaknesses, all our faults, but who likewise hearest the sighing of our contrite hearts, teach us who know but darkly and who see but a little way, to trust ourselves and all dear to us, without fear or doubt, to Thy never-failing love, that, with minds stayed on Thee, we may have perfect peace, in all our joys remembering Thee, in all our sorrows not cast down, and able through the bitterness of tears to say, "Thy will be done." Amen.[4]—Family Prayer

BLESSINGS NOW

- Pay attention to the admonition "Please, take good care of yourself." Listen to what your body "tells" you, and then wisely meet your requirements for a variety of healthful foods, adequate rest, and refreshing recreation.
- Accept your limitations as well as your abilities. Be courageous about adapting your lifestyle to fit your physical, emotional, and spiritual needs.
- Keep a wall calendar for tracking your fluctuating hormonal status, and hang it up in your closet or on the inside of your bathroom cupboard door. Show your husband how to refer to this convenient chart on days when he may be wondering what's up with you.

- Recognize and respect how your body functions by appreciating what it is, and isn't, capable of. Avoid comparing yourself to other women who may have more or less energy and stamina than you. Do what you can to stay healthy.
- Resolve never to complain about or criticize your appearance within your husband's range of hearing. Be confident in your attractiveness and desirability in his eyes.
- Go for the gold standard: Aim for a high quality of life by following these effective health guidelines:
  ◊ Drink plenty of water each day.
  ◊ Aim to include in your diet more foods rich in complex carbohydrates (whole grain products, fruits, and vegetables).
  ◊ Avoid too much sugar and saturated fats.
  ◊ Eat a variety of foods at every meal, including calcium- and protein-rich foods.
  ◊ Maintain a healthy weight.
  ◊ Read and memorize nutrition labels of your favorite foods.
  ◊ Invest in a comprehensive cookbook or food counter that contains nutrient charts and food exchanges.
  ◊ Get enough cardiovascular and strengthening exercise.
- Invite your husband to exercise regularly with you. Walking is especially ideal for this purpose. Whenever possible, adjust your pace and schedule to accommodate each other's needs.
- Stand naked in front of a full-length mirror in the privacy of your bathroom or bedroom; talk to yourself about what you see and how you feel about your body. Make peace with your appearance.

FOR FURTHER READING

Dan B. Allender and Tremper Longman III. *The Cry of the Soul: How Our Emotions Reveal Our Deepest Questions About God.* Colorado Springs: NavPress, 1999.

Lisa Bevere. *You Are Not What You Weigh.* Orlando, Fla.: Creation House, 1998.

Jill Briscoe. *The One Year Book of Quiet Times with God.* Wheaton, Ill.: Tyndale, 1997.

Oswald Chambers. *Devotions for a Deeper Life*. Grand Rapids: Zondervan, 1986.

Classics Devotional Bible. Grand Rapids: Zondervan, 1996.

Judith Couchman, comp. *One Holy Passion: Growing Deeper in Your Walk with God*. Colorado Springs: WaterBrook, 1998.

Debra Evans. *The Christian Woman's Guide to Personal Health Care*. Wheaton, Ill.: Crossway, 1998.

Archibald D. Hart and Catherine Hart Weber. *Unveiling Depression in Women: A Practical Guide to Understanding and Overcoming Depression*. Grand Rapids: Fleming H. Revell, 2002.

Gladys Hunt. *Honey for a Woman's Heart: Growing Your World Through Reading Great Books*. Grand Rapids: Zondervan, 2002.

Jean Lush. *Women and Stress*. Grand Rapids: Revell/Baker, 1992.

Andrew Murray. *Abide in Christ*. Uhrichsville, Ohio: Barbour & Co., 1992.

Henri J. M. Nouwen. *Making All Things New: An Invitation to the Spiritual Life*. New York: Harper & Row, 1981.

Stormie Omartian. *Finding Peace for Your Heart: A Woman's Guide to Emotional Health*. Nashville: Thomas Nelson, 1991.

Dónal O'Mathúna and Walt Larimore. *Alternative Medicine: The Christian Handbook*. Grand Rapids: Zondervan, 2001.

Charles Swindoll. *Growing Strong in the Seasons of Life*. Grand Rapids: Zondervan, 1983.

Ingrid Trobisch. *The Joy of Being a Woman*. New York: Harper & Row, 1975.

Walter Trobisch. *Love Yourself: Self-Acceptance and Depression*. Downers Grove, Ill.: InterVarsity, 1976.

SEVEN

The Blessings of Forgiveness and Mercy

A Christian will find it cheaper to pardon than to resent.
Forgiveness saves the expense of anger,
the cost of hatred, the waste of spirits.
HANNAH MORE (1745-1833)

Do you remember the often-quoted line from *Love Story?* "Love means never having to say you're sorry."

But this idealistic sentiment doesn't fit who we human beings really are. Love *does* mean having to say, "I'm sorry," and, even more important, "I forgive you." Jesus said in the Sermon on the Mount, "For if you forgive men when they sin against you, your heavenly Father will also forgive you. But if you do not forgive men their sins, your Father will not forgive your sins" (Matthew 6:14-15).

Building a home in which a family can bloom requires plenty of hard work on both sides. Learning to live "as one" isn't easy or natural for *anybody.*

Like most couples, neither David nor I had very realistic ideas about what we were getting ourselves into on the day we married. While some might say I was just "lucky" to find a man who would take his marriage vows seriously, I must be perfectly honest and say there were several times when both of us were ready to throw in the towel. Yet what would have been impossible for the two of us to accomplish on our own has become amazingly possible through Jesus Christ our Lord. Slowly but surely, day by day, our walk with God has revealed to us the blessings of His forgiveness and mercy, showing us how we may extend these blessings to one another. No human counselor would have had the ability to touch our hearts so deeply, supernaturally changing us from the inside out, teaching us how to love and serve one another, enabling us to keep going when we wanted to give up.

Like you, every day I find myself faced with an important set of choices and decisions regarding my marriage. It takes concentrated effort to keep my attention focused on what's most important: choosing to say *yes* to waiting upon the Lord and remembering His promises, and deciding to be thoughtful toward my husband, preparing my heart for our reunion at the end of the typically demanding day. Even when troubling problems arise or I've reached my stress limit, my husband needs and wants to be appreciated, desired, and cherished. Above all, he does not need or want me to repeatedly require him to earn my love. Without the blessings of forgiveness and mercy, meeting these needs and wants is impossible.

"Love's Power to Break Nature's Rule"

The intimate bond we share with our husbands tests us. Within the framework of marriage, we find that opposing needs, perspectives, desires, and personalities erode our self-centeredness. When we butt our heads up against one another's walls we get bruised. No matter how hard we try, remember, we can't love perfectly.

What can we do about all those bumps and bruises then? We can:
- Accept bruised feelings as an inevitable part of marriage and family life.
- Acknowledge our imperfections and be gracious about acknowledging them in our husband.

- Learn and practice the art of appropriate apology.
- Ease conflict through improved communication.
- Find ways to express our anger appropriately and fairly.
- Refuse to nurture feelings of self-pity, resentment, emotional dependency, and dissatisfaction.
- Be faithful in forgiving and extending mercy toward our husband.

"Forgiveness is God's invention for coming to terms with a world in which, despite their best intentions, people are unfair to each other and hurt each other deeply," notes theology professor Dr. Lewis Smedes. "He began by forgiving us. And he invites us all to forgive each other. Forgiving is love's toughest work, and love's biggest risk. If you twist it into something it was never meant to be, it can make you a doormat or an insufferable manipulator. Forgiving seems almost unnatural. Our sense of fairness tells us people should pay for the wrong they do. But forgiving is love's power to break nature's rule…. It is forgiving that supplies the healing stream of the long-term tomorrows."[1]

Love really does cover a "multitude of sins," keeping no record of wrongs suffered. It just isn't humanly possible to love this way. Still, while we can't love perfectly, we *can* choose to give up whatever at any given time is causing us to stumble in our attitude. It is our responsibility as Christians to persevere, keep moving on, and press toward our heavenly calling in Jesus.

Reach for the Goal

While it isn't always easy to keep "forgetting what is behind," once marital conflicts have been sufficiently resolved we need to make a conscious effort to turn away from the thoughts and memories that threaten to pull us away from "what is ahead." If you find yourself becoming discouraged in this regard, you can do several things to make it easier to keep moving forward:

Turn to the Bible for encouragement. Find passages that remind you of your eternal hope in Christ. Trust His ability to lead you each step of the way home. Encourage your faith by reading His Word, even when you would rather leave it on the shelf. Jesus wants you to be both whole and holy. Although you must wait until you meet Him to receive the fullness of all this means, your willingness to hear and obey His Word, by the power of the Holy Spirit, will bring you ever closer to this goal.

Share your concerns with the Lord in prayer. Don't be afraid to pour your heart out to God. "Blessed are the poor in spirit, for theirs is the kingdom of heaven" (Matthew 5:3). Ask the Lord to lead you, strengthen you, protect you, and sustain you by His Spirit. As your heart is drawn toward Christ and His kingdom, be encouraged by David's words: "Trust in him at all times, O people; pour out your hearts to him, for God is our refuge" (Psalm 62:8).

Talk to someone who is gifted in counseling. If you are having difficulty extending forgiveness to your husband or for some reason feel forgiveness is an inappropriate response to his behavior, ask your pastor to refer you to someone who will guard your privacy and give you sound advice and support.

✿ ✿ ✿ ────────────────────────────────

Not Perfect, but Possible

The solution to a fight, an argument, difference of opinion, unthoughtfulness on the part of another person, unfair treatment, selfishness, egoism, disregard for another person's rights, is not splitting up and finding other human beings to live with, but understanding what must be taught, time after time, through seeking to find solutions which are not perfect, but which are possible.

One lesson I tried to teach my children, from a very early age…was the fact that *some things must never be said, no matter how hot the argument, no matter how angry one becomes, no matter how far one goes in feeling, "I don't care how much I hurt him or her."* Some things are too much of a "luxury" ever to say. Some things are too great a price to pay for the momentary satisfaction of putting the other person down. Some things are like throwing indelible ink on a costly work of art, or smashing a priceless statue just to make a strong point in an argument. Saying certain things is an expense beyond all reason.

What is it that can never be put into words, which can't be erased and

Remember, time is one of the greatest sources of healing. The passage of time makes it increasingly more difficult to remember the specific details of past events and reminds us we are continually moving away from the occurrence of an offense or other harmful behavior. While it's true that every time you turn around and embrace the past you will rapidly recreate the feelings associated with it, it's also true that every step you take away from the source of your hurt will take you that much further from it.

Learning to say we're sorry and to extend forgiveness to each other is essential for marital peace. Each spouse needs to learn to develop the capacity for seeing beyond his or her own viewpoint in order to understand where the other is coming from. The next time you're tempted to "think small," try to envision the larger picture instead. We need steady discernment to determine what really matters in respect to

---

forgotten? What is it that one can resolve and succeed never to say during the lifetime of relationship with one person?

It is attacking the person in his or her most vulnerable, most sensitive, most insecure spot in life. It is pulling the rug out at a place where the other person felt there was solid acceptance and understanding, without question. It is bringing up something from the other person's background which he has no control over and which carries with it painful memories of outsiders' lack of understanding. It is turning the one secure place in all of life into a suddenly exposed place of naked attack from which there is no place to run. At some point in the beginning of a relationship, it is of tremendous importance to decide inside yourself just what things are really "out of bounds," and to declare to yourself that you will never resort to say anything about: his or her big nose, deformities, lack of cultural or educational upbringing, and psychological fears or special weaknesses. Naturally it can't be too big a list, but there must be certain specific areas you rationally decide not to let "wild horses drag out of you." It is possible. It is a restraint that you can inflict upon yourself. It is a possible control.[2]—Edith Schaeffer

✖ ✖ ✖

eternity. It becomes easier to do when we keep in mind who we are, why we're here, and where we're headed.

When you find yourself getting frustrated and fed up, recall what your husband most needs from you: your understanding, acceptance, and approval—not for what he has done or not done, but for who he *is*. Your husband needs you to rediscover your joy and delight in him, to see God's grand purposes for him, and to see the Lord's glorious image reflected in his face. He needs you to set healthy boundaries. He needs your tenderness, compassion, and care. He needs your patience. He needs your forgiveness. He needs your love.

From the Mercy We've Received

Blessing our husband out of the fullness of love we receive through Christ, the mediator of our marriage, opens our eyes to the power of God's Word to strengthen our spirit and set our heart free. Applying the wisdom and understanding we receive from the One who ordained marriage enables us to extend to our husband the forgiveness, comfort, encouragement, compassion, and peace we receive first from God.

When we withhold mercy, forgiveness, and understanding from our husband, our capacity to love and cherish him is diminished. We must be careful that our questions, comments, and actions don't become vehicles for expressing anger and hurtful put-downs to get the point across. The following verses clarify the biblical vision upon which we are to base our ideas about loving one another:

> Love must be sincere. Hate what is evil; cling to what is good.
> Be devoted to one another in brotherly love. Honor one
> another above yourselves. Never be lacking in zeal, but keep
> your spiritual fervor, serving the Lord. Be joyful in hope,
> patient in affliction, faithful in prayer. Share with God's people
> who are in need. Practice hospitality. Bless those who persecute
> you; bless and do not curse. Rejoice with those who rejoice;
> mourn with those who mourn. Live in harmony with one
> another. Do not be proud, but be willing to associate with

people of low position. Do not be conceited. Do not repay anyone evil for evil. Be careful to do what is right in the eyes of everybody. If it is possible, as far as it depends on you, live at peace with everyone. (Romans 12:9-18)

God's mercy toward us teaches us how we can be merciful toward our husband. In receiving God's love and forgiveness instead of His condemnation, we've been shown how to love and forgive one another. Resting upon the unchanging foundation of Christ's permanent love for us, our souls enjoy refreshment, peace, and strength in His quieting presence.

"To spiritually benefit from marriage, we have to be honest," says author Gary Thomas. "We have to look at our disappointments, own up to our ugly attitudes, and confront our selfishness. We also have to rid ourselves of the notion that the difficulties of marriage can be overcome if we simply pray harder or learn a few simple principles. Most of us have discovered that these 'simple steps' work only on a superficial level.

"Why is this? Because there's a deeper question that needs to be addressed beyond how we can 'improve' our marriage: What if God didn't design marriage to be 'easier'? What if God had an end in mind that went beyond our happiness, our comfort, and our desire to be infatuated and happy as if the world were a perfect place? *What if God designed marriage to make us holy more than to make us happy?*"[3]

We serve an almighty, living God who has given us many lasting promises on which to base our faith and hope. The Lord has shown us how to live out His calling for our life. We have concrete instructions that work; the choice to follow them is ours. Jesus has supplied us with a clearly marked map to lead our steps in the direction He wants them to go. If we choose to follow Him, we will experience life and freedom.

When we feel discouraged, we can choose to turn to God for wisdom and comfort. When we are in turmoil, we can ask Him to encourage us and bring us hope, reminding us of His grace. We can accept the freedom Christ alone offers us day by day through His renewing presence and unconditional love. As your marriage matures, I pray you will find the walls come tumbling down when you call on the Lord for help.

FOCUS POINTS

- When we withhold mercy, forgiveness, and understanding from our husband, our capacity to love and cherish them is diminished.
- Every day presents an important set of choices and decisions regarding our marriage. Even when troubling problems arise or we reach our stress limit, our husband needs and wants to be appreciated, desired, and cherished. If we won't give him the blessings of forgiveness and mercy, we will not be able to give him these other things either.
- Regardless of wrongs done to us, it is our responsibility as Christians to persevere, keep moving on, and press toward our heavenly calling in Jesus.
- Blessing our husband out of the fullness of love we receive through Christ, the mediator of our marriage, opens our eyes to the power of God's Word to strengthen our spirit and set our heart free.

WORDS TO REMEMBER

- Free me from the trap that is set for me, for you are my refuge. Into your hands I commit my spirit; redeem me, O LORD, the God of truth. (Psalm 31:4-5)
- Therefore, as God's chosen people, holy and dearly loved, clothe yourselves with compassion, kindness, humility, gentleness and patience. Bear with each other and forgive whatever grievances you may have against one another. Forgive as the Lord forgave you. (Colossians 3:12-13)
- You, my brothers, were called to be free. But do not use your freedom to indulge the sinful nature; rather, serve one another in love. The entire law is summed up in a single command: "Love your neighbor as yourself." If you keep on biting and devouring each other, watch out or you will be destroyed by each other. (Galatians 5:13-15)
- Create in me a pure heart, O God, and renew a steadfast spirit within me. (Psalm 51:10)

- As the Father has loved me, so have I loved you. Now remain in my love. (John 15:9)

REAL GUYS

"I find it amazingly graceful that my wife does not keep a track record of things I've done or said wrong in the past. When she forgives me, she forgives me. This makes me feel that she truly loves me and treasures me enough not to hurt me with things that have happened before."—Jason

PERSONAL REFLECTIONS

1. When you and your husband have an argument, what prevents you from forgiving one another? Write these things down and present your list to God, asking Him to remove or help you overcome these barriers in your marriage.
2. Complete the following thoughts in your journal:
   Taking a moral inventory of my life has shown me where I most need God to...
   Surrendering my whole heart to Jesus invites me to see and understand why...
   Loving my husband for who he is rather than who I want him to be requires...
3. What do you need to forgive your husband for today? In what ways does holding on to unforgiveness—even when the wrong done to you is real and painful—prevent you from moving into the fullness of God's purposes for your life?

PRAYERS

Praying God's Blessing for Our Marriage
   May all that we say and think be acceptable to you, Lord, our Rock and our Redeemer.—Psalm 19:14
Praying God's Blessing for My Husband
   Be my husband's rock of refuge, Lord, to which he can always go; give the command to save him, for you are his rock and his fortress.—Psalm 71:3

Closing Prayer

O Almighty God, give to Thy servant a meek and gentle spirit, that I may be slow to anger, and easy to mercy and forgiveness. Give me a wise and constant heart, that I may never be moved to an intemperate anger for any injury that is done or offered. Lord, let me ever be courteous, and easy to be entreated; let me never fall into a peevish or contentious spirit, but follow peace with all men; offering forgiveness, inviting them by courtesies, ready to confess my own errors, apt to make amends, and desirous to be reconciled. Let no sickness or cross accident, no employment or weariness, make me angry or ungentle or discontented, or unthankful, or uneasy to them that minister to me; but in all things make me like unto holy Jesus. Amen.[4]—Jeremy Taylor (1613-1667)

BLESSINGS NOW

- Decide not to try and get even with your husband for something he has said or done. Instead, do exactly the opposite: Forgive him, and keep moving on.
- Rely upon the Holy Spirit's strength, direction, and help as you pursue Christ's peace and obey His rule. "Get rid of all bitterness, rage and anger, brawling and slander, along with every form of malice. Be kind and compassionate to one another, forgiving each other, just as in Christ God forgave you" (Ephesians 4:31-32).
- Place a fresh rose in a vase by your bed the next time one of you forgives the other an offense. Consider making this colorful commemoration of your love a regular practice in your home.
- Call "Time Out": In the midst of a heated argument or escalating conflict, mutually agree to go your separate ways for at least thirty to sixty minutes. Chill. Calm yourself. Pray for patience and a larger perspective. Allow things to settle down before resuming your discussion.
- Elect not to go to bed and fall asleep if you're angry with your husband: Either take the time to talk with him about how you feel or tell God all about it in prayer.

- Say or do something kind for your husband in the wake of an apology or settled dispute.
- Seek God's wisdom and understanding; vigorously apply His truth to your heart, mind, and soul. Extend to your husband the forgiveness, comfort, encouragement, compassion, and peace you receive first from God.
- Determine in advance that the satisfying times in your marriage are worth making it through the disappointing times. In the midst of difficulty, stay focused on the big picture.
- Ask God to enable your love for your husband to grow deeper when you hit a brick wall. If you can't climb over the problem, plow under it. With the Holy Spirit's help:
  ◊ Accept bruised feelings as an inevitable part of marriage and family life.
  ◊ Acknowledge your imperfections and be gracious about acknowledging them in your husband.
  ◊ Learn and practice the art of appropriate apology.
  ◊ Seek ways to improve your communication.
  ◊ Find ways to express your anger appropriately and fairly.
  ◊ Refuse to nurture feelings of self-pity, resentment, emotional dependency, and dissatisfaction.
  ◊ Be faithful in forgiving and extending mercy toward your husband.
- Do your part to make your marriage the best it can be. If you do this, you will not look back with regret from the vantage point of eternity.

For Further Reading

Kay Arthur. *Lord, Heal My Hurts*. Portland, Ore.: Multnomah, 1989.

David Augsburger. *The Freedom of Forgiveness*. Chicago: Moody, 1970.

Jerry Bridges. *Transforming Grace*. Colorado Springs: NavPress, 1991.

Dwight Carlson. *Overcoming Hurts and Anger.* Eugene, Ore.: Harvest House, 2000.

Bill and Pam Farrel. *Love, Honor & Forgive: A Guide for Married Couples.* Downers Grove, Ill.: InterVarsity, 2000.

John Gottman, with Nan Silver. *The Seven Principles for Making Marriage Work.* New York: Three Rivers, 1999.

Joyce Huggett. *Listening to Others.* Downers Grove, Ill.: InterVarsity, 1988.

C. S. Lewis. *The Four Loves.* London: Geoffrey Bles, 1960.

Brennan Manning. *The Wisdom of Tenderness: What Happens When God's Fierce Mercy Transforms Our Lives.* San Francisco: Harper-SanFrancisco, 2002.

John Nieder and Thomas M. Thompson. *Forgive and Love Again: Healing Wounded Relationships.* Eugene, Ore.: Harvest House, 1991.

Gary Rosberg. *The Do-It-Yourself Relationship Mender: A Remarkable Remedy for Unresolved Conflict.* Colorado Springs: Focus on the Family, 1992, 1995.

M. Basilea Schlink. *Repentance: The Joy-filled Life.* Grand Rapids: Zondervan, 1968.

Lewis Smedes. *The Art of Forgiving.* Nashville: Moorings, 1996.

Lewis Smedes. *Forgive and Forget.* San Francisco: Harper & Row, 1984.

Leslie Vernick. *How to Act Right When Your Spouse Acts Wrong.* Colorado Springs: WaterBrook, 2001.

EIGHT

The Blessings of Friendship and Tenderness

❧

Life is war, and marriage provides us with a close and intimate ally with whom we may wage this war.
DAN ALLENDER AND TREMPER LONGMAN III

I once met an unusual couple in a childbirth class I was teaching. They were in their forties and expecting their eighth child. Out of the thousands of men and women I have had the privilege to work with, this particular couple stands out as a memorable example of a husband and wife wholly devoted to one another.

They were like a couple of teenagers. They would laugh and tickle one another during the exercises, hold hands during breaks, and act just as interested in learning about giving birth for the eighth time as they probably were for the first. Here was a couple old enough to be grandparents, with a daughter in her sophomore year of college; yet they acted as if the entire process of childbearing were completely new.

On the fourth night of class, I asked these two best friends what their secret was. The wife smiled as she glanced over at her husband,

and they both began to give me the same answer simultaneously. It turned out that ever since they had begun dating, they spent Friday nights out together. After they married, they kept up the tradition. "Even if it's just to go for a half-hour walk, Bob and I make sure we have time alone," she explained. "He makes me feel just like I used to before I married him by always taking that time out for me."

Early in their marriage, this couple had learned an invaluable lesson: Marriage is the most important human relationship a man and a woman voluntarily commit to in love. It was designed to survive raising kids to adulthood and all of the stresses and strains involved in family life.

Obviously, the marriage friendship doesn't just automatically outlast all of these things. It must be lovingly nourished if it's to handle the demands placed upon it.

Ezer-more

When you hear the word *companion*, what does the term signify to you? Given the dictionary's definition of a companion as "somebody who accompanies you, spends time with you, or is a friend," do you currently see you and your husband companionably drawing together or separately drifting apart? Author Sheldon Vanauken warns:

> There is such as thing as a creeping separateness. What do young people who are freshly married do? They can't rest when they're apart. They want to be together all the time. But they develop separate interests, especially if they have separate jobs and some separate friends. So they drift apart. Pretty soon they have little in common except, maybe, the children. So the stage is set for one of them to fall in love with someone else. Later they'll say the reason for the divorce was that he/she fell in love with someone else, but it wasn't that at all. It was because they let themselves grow apart.[1]

In Genesis 2:18, we hear these words echo across the centuries, still vitally relevant to our relationships today: "The LORD God said,

'It is not good for the man to be alone. I will make a helper suitable for him.' " Consider that the Hebrew word for helper is *ezer*—remarkably, the same word used in Psalm 118:7: "The LORD is with me; he is my helper (*ezer*)." Keeping this idea in mind reinforces the essential role we play within our sacred partnership. The blessing of friendship and tenderness in marriage honors this unchanging truth: *A wife's loving companionship was designed by God to meet her husband's number-one earthly relationship need.*

Evaluate your level of intimacy with your husband, then consider whether you might have been neglecting your husband's needs for affection, comfort, and camaraderie. Ask your husband what he would like to experience with you in this area. Talk about your observations with each other. Reflect on times you have felt closest to your husband—what made the difference? What are your expectations concerning your husband's friendship today? Is spending time with him fulfilling or disappointing? Why?

Have you had a night or weekend away alone together in the past year? What about the possibility of setting up regularly scheduled dates so you can spend time giving one another your undivided attention? If your husband seems less energized about this idea than you are, go back to the drawing board: Keep praying, asking for God's guidance and wisdom about how your marriage friendship can best be strengthened and renewed right now.

Whether you prefer a special night out that involves dressing up and making reservations at an exclusive restaurant, or an evening of fishing in a canoe, spending time together is what counts. Getting out alone, away from the dishes, the laundry, the bills, and the kids—even for a brief time—can do your relationship a world of good. The ideas in Appendix 8.1, "101 Great Dates," will give you a place to start. It may seem like a big effort at first, especially if you're not used to spending a few hours a week away from work and family responsibilities. But I encourage you to make this effort: As your bond is renewed by your commitment to regularly schedule time alone together, your entire relationship will likely be refreshed.

Don't be discouraged if you meet with some resistance from your husband at first. Plenty of couples struggle with their "what I want to do tonight" differences. Outside the bedroom, it isn't always easy to find common ground in which to plant the seeds of marital intimacy and friendship. Even so, be patient; please don't give up. In time, you likely will reap a colorful harvest.

Discovery in Our Differences

At this point you may be wondering whether the effort will be worth it. While I can't make any absolute promises, I can speak from my own three-decades-plus experience. Here's why: My husband and I began our married life together without any shared hobbies and with many divergent interests: He wanted to go to baseball games; I preferred going to the ballet. I was an avid reader; he spent most of his free time playing basketball or the guitar. He rarely stepped foot inside the

❦ ❦ ❦ —————————————————————————————

Becoming Soul Mates

We hope you and your spouse are at the stage of deeply wanting to be soul mates—if indeed you haven't already formed such a bond. To begin with, soul mates have much more than a physical and emotional bond. They develop an ongoing, growing, spiritual dimension to their relationship. They come to realize that they will not excel in their marriage unless God is present and active in their lives. They keep learning and relearning that marriage is a spiritual task and their perspective is to "know and serve God" and "produce Christ in my partner at every turn."

Embracing God together involves spontaneity and structure. Get to a place when you have time for prayers, Scripture reading, praise and worship, meditation, service, and more. Go slow if you have to, but do it. And remember, there is no perfect style.

Some helpful hints we use:

• Stay focused on your purpose.

• Come to God with a spirit of expectancy.

• Don't set each other up for failure by trying to do too much (such as

house if the sun was shining; I thrived indoors, regardless of the weather. And so on and so forth.

After we celebrated our first anniversary, I wondered if we had enough in common to make our marriage work. Initially, our mutual attraction to one another *had* been enough. Clearly, we needed something more to strengthen and deepen our bond.

Even though I was uncertain about the outcome, I began praying. I asked God to strengthen our marriage and opened my heart to His leading in the daily details of our married life together. Though I am still learning (and praying), I can now look back over the years and see a beautiful theme emerging: In learning to respect and even appreciate one another's differences, my husband and I no longer feel threatened by those parts of ourselves that are "apart," or different, from each other. Because both of us have repeatedly been willing to go outside our

---

reading thirty chapters of the Bible a day) on activities that don't work well for the two of you (like forcing devotions when kids are screaming and your eyes don't open until 10:00 A.M.!).

• Don't be critical of each other's efforts.

• Don't quit!

The concept of "two becoming one" is no longer seen as an occasional coupling. Instead, neither spouse feels quite complete without the other one. As wonderful as the mating part of marriage might have been, the soul-mating stage is even more special. It provides a permanence to the spiritual intimacy. The spouses' lives take on a shared meaning.

They also revel in the shared journey they are making together.... It's no longer two individuals involved in competition and evaluation of one another. By now each is just as sincerely concerned about the other spouse's growth as about his or her own. They're in this marriage together, and they're in it for the long haul.

Communion with God. A shared meaning. A shared journey. Those are the basics of becoming soul mates.[2]—Timothy and Julie Clinton

❀ ❀ ❀

dissimilar comfort zones—he occasionally attending the ballet or "chick flick" with me; I going to see baseball/football/basketball/hockey games with him, for example—our well-weathered companionship has become more interesting and richly textured, allowing us both to grow together as a couple and as individuals. The blessing of friendship—the willingness to prefer my husband's companionship above all others—has helped me be more tender toward the man I now know better and appreciate more than anyone else in the world.

A High-Yield Investment

Marital friendship thrives with the companionship, shelter, and support we give our husband. Like a garden, a strong bond between a wife and her husband cannot be created without careful planning and nurture; this friendship must be wisely tended, watered, weeded, and harvested. Done well, these responsibilities require a generous investment of time, effort, and energy. A superb garden does not blossom overnight. To produce and maintain a durable friendship with our husband, we need to be willing to spend quality time in ample quantity.

Jesus affirmed, "For where your treasure is, there your heart will be also" (Matthew 6:21). Husbands know when their wives treasure them. They see it in our eyes, hear it in our voice, feel it in our touch, and sense it in our presence. When we honor our husband with our time, attention, and presence, he knows we highly esteem and sincerely value him. In this way, we give him the opportunity to understand why his feelings, passions, life experiences, and well-being matter to us. Above all, we invite him to trust that our love for him is nonnegotiable.

Think back to a time when a friend gave you the gift of her time, attention, and comfort. How did you feel? What did she do or say that was especially meaningful to you? Can you explain the qualities you most appreciated about her?

Our best friends know our likes and dislikes. Though they are quite familiar with our idiosyncrasies, shortcomings, and bad habits, they choose to focus on and nurture our unique strengths and talents. When they speak the truth to us in love, we usually listen. And so it is with husbands. The main point, I believe, is to make the wisest choices we can about the amount of time and energy necessary to bring about the desired result.

Over the years, meeting your husband's God-made need for physical, emotional, and spiritual connection with you will require a certain amount of flexibility, patience, and understanding. It isn't always feasible to get away together when increased job responsibilities, marital conflict, an illness, family demands, active military duty, or other life challenges temporarily preclude your regular time together. In such situations, make use of supplementary strategies as a means of nourishing your bond. Sometimes, just silently sitting side by side is enough. When you're apart, liberally use phone calls, e-mail, faxes, and letters to remain close and convey your blessing across the miles.

Changing seasons across the course of one's lifetime can teach vital lessons about the nature of love and true friendship. As you grow in your ability to nurture your friendship with your mate, you will learn many practical ways to express your love for him while considering his needs and paying attention to his personal preferences.

"I am fully, totally married to my wife," says Bob, married for thirty years. "When I am alone, physically or emotionally, I am uncomfortable. A part of me is 'missing.' My wife knows this, and we have always concentrated on maintaining a connection. When we pray, I know that her hand is reaching to touch mine. When we lie down to sleep, even after one of those episodes where we don't see each other's side of a controversy, we find our feet gliding through the sheets to touch gently. All is well, and we can go to sleep.

"Our thirty-year marriage has continued to get stronger as we both have allowed ourselves to be weak alone, and to be complete only through our love for each other. Her simple touch, no words necessary, says it all."

The blessing of friendship and tenderness is a priceless gift. Husbands who have received it from their wife say that nothing else compares with the kind of intimate companionship only their wife supplies. Wives who have given it smile with satisfaction when asked to describe what they like most about their relationship with their husband. It is a friendship worth nourishing and cultivating.

FOCUS POINTS

- Marriage is the most important human relationship a man and a woman voluntarily commit to in love. It was designed to survive raising kids to adulthood and all of the stresses and strains involved in family life. In order to succeed, however, the friendship a husband and wife share must be lovingly nourished.

- The blessing of friendship in marriage—the willingness to prefer our husband's companionship above all others—honors this unchanging truth: A wife's loving companionship was designed by God to meet her husband's number-one relationship need.

- Over the years, meeting our husband's God-made need for physical, emotional, and spiritual connection with us will require a certain amount of flexibility, patience, and understanding. As we grow in our ability to nurture our friendship with our mate, we will learn practical ways to express our love for him while considering his needs and paying attention to his personal preferences.

WORDS TO REMEMBER

- Then God said, "Let us make man in our image, in our likeness, and let them rule over the fish of the sea and the birds of the air, over the livestock, over all the earth, and over all the creatures that move along the ground." So God created man in his own image, in the image of God he created him; male and female he created them. (Genesis 1:26-27)

- My command is this: Love each other as I have loved you. Greater love has no one than this, that he lay down his life for his friends. (John 15:12-13)

- A wife of noble character who can find? She is worth far more than rubies. Her husband has full confidence in her and lacks nothing of value. (Proverbs 31:10-11)

- Therefore what God has joined together, let man not separate. (Matthew 19:6b)

REAL GUYS

"Opposites attract. Lorilee and I were a classic case of country boy meets city girl. However, sometimes opposites are, well, opposite. Big city lights tend to give this country boy a migraine, and the sight of one nice, juicy fishing worm induces an eerie, silent catatonia in my city girl. So it is sometimes difficult for both of us to make the kinds of gestures that value the other for who we are at the core: country boy, city girl. But Lorilee has found a gesture that does just that.

"Lorilee is what you might call a word junkie. When she is not writing books, magazine articles, news features, or cover copy, she can usually be found hiding somewhere quiet, reading a book. On gift-giving occasions and compulsive book-buying sprees in general, she has a knack for picking out books that really resonate with my interests, books that I would never have found on my own: books about the history of the cod-fishing industry, books about death in the wilderness, books about the perfect catfish bait, books about obscure country blues singers—books she would never be interested in herself. This shows me that she loves me for who I am, oddball interests and obsessions and all.

"Now if I could only get her to share my appreciation for the beauty of an unmowed lawn in full bloom."—Doyle

PERSONAL REFLECTIONS

1. What kind of "creeping separateness" are you and your husband most susceptible to? What steps can you take toward one another to close the gap? Ask a close friend to help you with some creative problem-solving if you have to work around obstacles like unusual work hours and sleeping patterns, careers that require travel, and other demands.
2. Complete these thoughts in your journal:
   From my husband's point of view, a close companion would be...
   Something we haven't done together for a long time that we once enjoyed is...
   When my husband and I are close, I feel...

3. Do you notice a difference in your husband when your companionship is in a healthy place versus when you are drifting?
In what ways? In what ways are you personally different when
the two of you are close?

PRAYERS

Praying God's Blessing for Our Marriage

Let the words of Christ, in all their richness, live in our hearts and
make us wise. May we use his words to teach and counsel each
other.—Colossians 3:16

Praying God's Blessing for My Husband

May my husband receive from you all wisdom and spiritual understanding for full insight into your will, Lord, so that his manner of life
may be worthy of you, and entirely pleasing to you.—Colossians 1:9-10

Closing Prayer

O LORD our God, teach us, we beseech Thee, to ask for the right
blessings. Steer Thou the vessel of our life toward Thyself, Thou tranquil
Haven of all storm-tossed souls. Show us the course wherein we should
go. Renew a willing spirit within us. Let Thy Spirit curb our wayward
senses, and guide and enable us unto that which is our true good, to keep
Thy laws, and in all our works evermore to rejoice in Thy glorious and
gladdening presence. For Thine is the glory and the praise from all Thy
saints forever and ever. Amen.[3]—Basil of Caesarea (330-379)

BLESSINGS NOW

- Invest your time, attention, and energy wisely; treasure your
husband's companionship above all others.
- Communicate and touch your husband tenderly, from your
heart. Convey your affection for him with verbal and nonver-
bal expressions of your care and concern for him, affirming
and reassuring him of your love in a variety of ways: Smile,
take his hand, blow him a kiss, stroke his neck, nibble his
neck, say something outrageously intimate, say something
intriguingly mysterious, say please and thank you, snuggle, lie
together skin-to-skin, curl up together on the couch fully
clothed, hold him in your arms when you wake up in the

morning, leave him a brief and loving voice-mail message at work midday, wish him good night and sweet dreams before falling asleep, and give him regular back rubs. (And teach him how to return the favor! See Appendix 8.2 for tips on how to give a great back rub.)

• With your husband's help and input, jointly set aside time for being out together at least once a week. Build this appointment into your schedule as a regular, ongoing event.

• Be faithful and true to your husband; practice emotional as well as physical fidelity.

• Go outside your comfort zone. Share with your husband an experience that isn't currently on your radar screen. Ask him to do the planning based on one of his favorite interests. By keeping an open mind, you'll likely learn a lot from this alien adventure.

• Celebrate not just your wedding anniversary, but other important shared dates and milestones as well:

   ◊ Send your husband a card at work to commemorate the day you met him.

   ◊ Clip a postcard on his car visor as a reminder of a favorite vacation spot. Write a note on the card reminiscing about a time you spent there together.

   ◊ Give him weekly, end-of-the-year thank-you notes expressing your appreciation for him between Thanksgiving and New Year's Day.

   ◊ Keep a couple's prayer journal your husband will enjoy reading, filled with praises, requests, Scripture verses, quotes, blessings, and thanks to God.

• Play hooky: Cancel a meeting, skip a class, reschedule an appointment. Arrange a rendezvous with your husband at a time when you normally wouldn't be together.

• Enjoy the blessings of low-key companionship when you're too tired to actively interact with one another: Read, watch TV, take a nap, listen to music, silently share a meal, sit out on the deck or porch sipping iced tea, go for a quiet walk in the cool of the evening. No pressure. No agenda. No big deal. Just being together can have a soothing effect on your marriage friendship.

• Write a delicious love note and place it inside your husband's dinner napkin, briefcase, pants pocket, sack lunch, checkbook, or coffee cup.

• Reminisce about your friendship. Get out your favorite photo books, view some old videos, look at your wedding pictures. Recall the years gone by to gain greater perspective on the marital territory you've recently been traveling through together as well as the road ahead.

FOR FURTHER READING

Timothy and Julie Clinton. *The Marriage You've Always Wanted.* Nashville: Word, 2000.

Robert and Pamela Crosby. *Creative Conversation Starters for Couples.* Tulsa, Okla.: Honor, 2000.

James and Shirley Dobson. *Night Light: A Devotional for Couples.* Sisters, Ore.: Multnomah, 2000.

David and Theresa Ferguson; Chris and Holly Thurman. *Intimate Encounters: A Practical Guide to Discovering the Secrets of a Really Great Marriage.* Nashville: Thomas Nelson, 1994.

Bill and Lyndi McCartney; Connie Neal. *Sold Out Two-Gether: A Couples Workbook.* Nashville: Word, 1999.

Les and Leslie Parrott. *Becoming Soul Mates.* Grand Rapids: Zondervan, 1995.

Dennis and Barbara Rainey. *Moments Together for Couples.* Ventura, Calif.: Regal, 1995.

Gary and Barbara Rosberg. *The Five Love Needs of Men and Women.* Wheaton, Ill.: Tyndale, 2000.

Gary Smalley. *Secrets to Lasting Love.* New York: Simon & Schuster, 2000.

Gary and Norma Smalley. *It Takes Two to Tango: More than 250 Secrets to Communication, Romance and Intimacy in Marriage.* Colorado Springs: Focus on the Family, 1997.

Gary Smalley and John Trent. *The Language of Love.* New York: Pocket, 1988.

Nick and Nancy Stinnett; Donnie Hilliard. *Magnificent Marriage: 10 Beacons Show the Way to Marriage Happiness.* West Monroe, La.: Howard Publishing, 2000.

Neil Clark Warren. *The Triumphant Marriage: 100 Extremely Successful Couples Reveal Their Secrets.* Colorado Springs: Focus on the Family, 1995.

H. Norman Wright. *Communication: Key to Your Marriage.* Ventura, Calif.: Regal, 2000.

H. Norman Wright. *Holding on to Romance.* Ventura, Calif.: Regal, 1992.

NINE

The Blessings of Lovemaking

❦

Real sex in real life is not so much a performance,
what you do, as a method of communication,
what you are attempting to say.
JOYCE HUGGETT

*L*ove communicated to our husband through our sexual design is an elegant, even sacred, language, involving our whole body, mind, and spirit. When we tenderly kiss our husband or willingly join our body with his in lovemaking, a most intimate conversation takes place, strengthening the bond we share, informing us of our love for one another, and reminding us of the one-flesh mystery within marriage.

Becoming familiar with the language of lovemaking takes time—and much patience—as we face our fears and eventually become fluent in ways of intimately expressing and sharing ourself with our husband. Because our sexuality is made up of so much more than our physical actions, the dialog we progressively develop in marriage becomes our own unique form of communication, distinctively informing our mate about who we are.

As women, God has given us the ability to be sexually expressive and creatively responsive when we feel loved, protected, and accepted by our husband. In bringing our uncovered selves to the marriage bed, we sooner or later discover why engaging in lovemaking out of a sense of duty alone doesn't make sense: Sexual intimacy seems intentionally designed by our Maker to be a savory source of physical and emotional satisfaction for *both* spouses. Is it any wonder that genuine fulfillment on all these levels occurs only when we resist the urge to manage/control/manipulate our responses, let go, and simply *enjoy* the way God has designed our body?

Comfortable with Our Uniqueness

Mutual satisfaction in lovemaking isn't possible when one or both partners isn't comfortable with being sexually responsive. Unless we learn how to feel comfortable with our body and can lovingly guide our husband as we teach him to view our needs from a woman's perspective, we may wonder why others consider sex such a great thing. Sex may seem like something done *to us* rather than something *we do*. This discomfort is not a threat to be ignored, stuffed down, or forgotten. Rather, we can view it as a golden opportunity to discover the source of what we're feeling and sensing.

Lori, a participant in one of my classes, once shared with me her frustration concerning sexual intimacy. She started by saying she didn't like that her husband had a tendency to head straight for her erogenous zones almost every time they touched. Often she tried to redirect his hands, hinting at possible alternatives to his approach. Though Lori wasn't sure what she wanted, she chose not to say anything to her spouse because she thought he should know what she wanted. If he didn't, he would figure it out someday. Talk about a vicious cycle!

Lori also voiced concern that she typically hurried through lovemaking because she was often too tense or upset with her husband's intense focus on sex to enjoy their times in bed together. Whenever her husband asked, "What's wrong, honey?" Lori said she simply told him everything was fine or turned her back to him, stuffing down her anger and frustration.

"I'm starting to think it's useless to talk about my needs with my husband when I've already told him how I feel," Lori confessed. "On the other hand, I'm not sure whether we're having trouble because he's not listening or because I'm not clearly communicating with him about my frustration level."

I think many of us can relate to Lori's situation. When it comes to expressing and sharing sexual intimacy with our husband, a big question we all face is: *What do we need, expect, want, or desire?*

It's safe to assume that many, if not most, women often want to be lovingly stroked, caressed, and embraced skin-to-skin before, during, and after lovemaking. Sometimes, what we want (and need) is simply a nurturing back rub, without feeling pressured to initiate or respond to our husband's eagerness for lovemaking. At other times, we very much want to make love with passionate abandon. Still at others, what we desire is just to hold hands with our husband and talk for a while, to reconnect face-to-face after a long, demanding day. But, unless we express what we need and want in terms of sexual and emotional intimacy, how will our husband know what we're thinking and feeling? As a result, he may rush into things too quickly or make assumptions that end up turning us off or hurting our feelings. He may also be more likely to turn over and fall asleep after lovemaking, leaving us alone to ponder the meaning of it all in the dark.

Don't be afraid to evaluate your level of intimacy; find ways to share what is on your mind. (See Appendix 9.1: "Are You Avoiding Your Husband?") What are your expectations concerning your sexual relationship with your husband? Is making love with him disappointing? Why? Think about the times when your arousal was totally unplanned and spontaneous—what made the difference? After thinking about these questions, you may find it helpful to discuss your concerns with your husband. On the other hand, you may also be ready to make some positive changes without much preliminary discussion.

Each woman needs to discover her own preferences instead of expecting to react as a textbook case. Because every woman experiences sexual and emotional intimacy in her own way, we need to feel comfortable sharing our thoughts and feelings about sex with our husband if lovemaking is to be mutually satisfying. The solution lies in our willingness to take responsibility for exploring and expressing our varying reactions to sex—and our husband's willingness to keep listening.

Whole Again

Because we receive God's good gift of our sexuality in the midst of a fallen world, we can't escape the necessity of confronting our sin and imperfection within the sexual dimension of marriage. As a result, God calls us to courageously refuse to pretend the past—and the present—doesn't matter. Instead, He invites us to wholeheartedly embrace His unfailing love and forgiveness as He heals and remakes our heart.

We frequently view our husband as the cause of our conflicting, self-protective feelings and impulses. Even though we know that no human being is capable of completely meeting our needs, we may not fully accept this fact. Over time we may harden our heart against him, structuring our times of sexual union according to some sort of predictable schedule so as to avoid self-exposure or rejection. After all, when we're hurting, we want to remain in control. This is where another vicious cycle starts: Resentment, bitterness, or despair transform lovemaking into one more burden we must bear rather than the gift of God it actually is.

Let's face it: All of us have been affected by sexual sin in one way or another. Few women have not been touched in a sexual way by someone other than our husband; fewer still have never fantasized nor thought about another person in sexual terms. It has been estimated that between 25 and 38 percent of women living in the United States today have experienced sexual abuse or assault.[1] Millions more of us have experienced divorce, directly or indirectly. What's more, countless Christian wives must face the consequences of their husband's involvement with pornography, sexual addiction, homosexuality, Internet liaisons, or an extramarital affair.

Some of us have felt, at one time or another, as if we'll never be whole again or able to make love expressively, from the heart, with our husband. Because we doubt we've been completely forgiven in Christ, we hold back from sharing ourself openly with our spouse. Because we associate painful or confusing memories from our past with sexual intimacy, we may also carry anger, hurt, fear, shame, resentment, or guilt as leftover baggage.

These emotions and experiences directly impact our desire and ability to welcome our husband to the marriage bed. If we don't feel we can trust our husband with our body, or if we're intimidated, annoyed, or ashamed by the associations we have with sexual pleasure and intimacy, we'll feel torn between wanting to hide and wanting to be intimate.

When we close the door on the Lord and shut Him out of this area of our life, we lock ourselves into feeling condemned, cheated, and wronged. If we stay stuck long enough, eventually an affair ("I was only looking for affection"), divorce ("If I just had another chance, things would be okay again"), or retribution ("He's going to pay for this") may seem a more appealing, less painful alternative to being made whole again.

Jesus offers a different way out. *If our desire is to love our husband and honor the Lord, He will lead us into sexual wholeness.* Through Christ, we're given the opportunity to be made new in *every* area of our life. It's almost unbelievable. To feel dead or empty inside and then discover the path of eternal life and freedom is like a dream come true. We hear the words, we read God's Word, yet we may still not believe it. Even so, God has promised to recreate and restore us through His Holy Spirit's steadfast work.

I'm not saying this transformation will be easy or instantaneous. Be that as it may, all it takes to get started is this simple prayer: "Yes, Lord, here I am. I give You my mind, my heart, my body, my spirit, my will, and my life. You are all that I need. Jesus, I'm Yours."

If you're having difficulty with sexual arousal and responsiveness in your marriage, please don't discount your emotional discomfort. It's there for a good reason, if only as an indicator that you need a temporary time out from sexual interaction due to stress or seasonal changes in your life. If your uneasiness with lovemaking continues for several weeks or longer, seek God's wisdom and discernment concerning how to respond to your current circumstances. Consider consulting a Christ-centered counselor, preferably a woman, who may help you understand your feelings about your body's reactions to sexual arousal. Don't worry; you're not abnormal. Nor are you alone. Literally millions of women have struggled with similar feelings.

You and your husband both have the responsibility to discuss your ideas, concerns, and preferences before engaging in any sexual activity that might cause either of you to experience discomfort, shame, or embarrassment. By accepting this responsibility together, it will be possible for the two of you to develop many creative approaches to lovemaking with one another.

Above all, be confident in the Lord's ability to *cleanse, heal,* and *restore* you as you are gradually transformed by the renewing of your mind and conformed to Christ's image. As you face your fear and brokenness with the Holy Spirit's help, you will discover God's merciful design for your life in all of its liberating fullness.

Mutual Satisfaction

"Sexual disclosure and vulnerability open spouses up to deeper self-knowledge," assert Fuller Theological Seminary professors Judith S. Balswick and Jack O. Balswick in *Authentic Human Sexuality.* "The

❧ ❧ ❧ ───────────────────────────────

When Happiness Goes Away

Marriage is a lot of hard work, period. I don't know of anyone who has been married very long who does not attest to that. When couples do the right kind of work—character work—they find that they can gain more happiness in their marriage than they thought possible. But it always comes as the result of going through some difficult moments. Conflicts, fears, and old traumas. Big and small rejections, arguments, and hurt feelings. The disillusionment of someone being different than one imagines. The difficult task of accepting imperfections and immaturity that are larger than one thinks they should be.

All of these things are normal, and all of these things are workable. And if people work through them, they reach happiness again, usually a happiness of a deeper and better sort. But if they hit these inevitable walls and have the attitude that this problem is "interfering with my happiness," they are in trouble. They will be angry with the "inconvenience" of their happi-

ability to know and be known as spouses requires an emotional and sexual exposure in which intimacy flourishes. We believe that every couple must find a balance between [emotional and sexual] intimacy in order to blend them in mutually satisfying ways. Women may need to stretch themselves in sexual areas, whereas men may need to challenge themselves in the emotional dimension. When emotional intimacy is lacking, the sexual appetite usually deteriorates, and when the sexual relationship is lacking, the emotional connection diminishes.

"A couple can have the best of both worlds by attending to both aspects of intimacy. The erotic energy moves spouses toward deep emotional connection that enhances erotic expression. When women take greater responsibility for their sexual satisfaction and men make a stronger link between sexual and emotional intimacy, they say yes to couple intimacy."[2]

Yes! We've been given the freedom to say yes to the gift of our sexuality within the holy bond of marriage. By giving ourself permission to

---

ness being interrupted and will refuse to solve the issues or will just leave the relationship. If happiness is our guide and it goes away momentarily, we will assume that something is wrong.

The truth is . . . that when we are not happy, something good may be happening. You may have been brought to that moment of crisis because of a need for growth, and that crisis may be the solution to much of what is wrong with your life. If you could grasp whatever it is that the situation is asking you to learn, it could change your entire life. . . .

When loving God is our orienting principle in life, we are always adjusting to what he requires from us. When things get tough in a marriage and when some change is required from us, we may not want to do it. We might feel that it is unfair that we have to change, or it might be too difficult or painful to change. At these moments, it is much easier to just please ourselves. But if we know that it's God with whom we ultimately have to deal, we submit to this reality and his higher call for us to grow. In the end, the relationship wins.[3]—Dr. Henry Cloud and Dr. John Townsend

❦ ❦ ❦

face the concerns and questions we hold in our heart about sexuality, we're better able to speak articulately with our body and experience real enjoyment. It's when we stop trying to be what we're not and accept our own unique styles of sexual response that we begin to understand the tremendous range of expression we are capable of: shouting, whispering, chatting, enunciating, crying out—a woman's body speaks in all these different ways.

Consider the areas of your body specifically created for expressing sexual intimacy. Do you feel comfortable thinking about them? Do you enjoy sharing these areas with your husband? Are you familiar enough with your body to use it to speak expressively to your husband?

The next time you are with your husband in bed, notice how your body responds to and communicates with him. As you become better acquainted with your body, why not become more familiar with your husband's body as well? Ask him to show you how he likes to be stroked and kissed. What areas does he say are the most sensitive? What types of touch give him the most pleasure? Notice the texture of skin on the different areas of his body. As you consider the ways his body complements yours, what impresses you most about your differences? Your similarities? What positive feelings do you have about your husband's body? Is there anything about his physical form that positively delights you?

Spend time with the worksheet in Appendix 9.2 for more suggestions on how to encourage sexual intimacy with your husband.

The purpose of our sexuality is to promote unity, or oneness, within marriage. This oneness comes not only through the act of making love, but in our ongoing respect for keeping God's rules and our mutual high regard for one another—our different growth patterns, emotional needs, bodily experiences, spiritual makeup, and personal vulnerabilities.

Our sexual relationship with our husband is worth nurturing, protecting, improving, honoring, praying for, celebrating, encouraging, appreciating, paying attention to, and enjoying. As Christ's followers, may our hope be that we may express our sexuality in mutually satisfying ways with our husband, facing the challenges that come our way with grace and wisdom. By acknowledging the beauty of God's natural design for sexuality within marriage—and also refusing to close our eyes to the effects of sexual sin and brokenness—may we find an increasing measure of peace, wonder, and joy in this most private area of our lives together.

FOCUS POINTS

- Becoming familiar with the language of lovemaking takes time—and much patience—as we face our fears and eventually become fluent in ways of expressing and sharing our sexuality with our husband.
- Our body doesn't respond willingly without our wholehearted emotional assent. With this internal voice of approval, we're more likely to find ourselves enjoying intimate times with our husband.
- You and your husband both have the right—and the responsibility—to discuss your ideas and preferences before engaging in any sexual activity that might cause either of you to experience discomfort, shame, or embarrassment. In this fashion, you can together develop many creative approaches to lovemaking.
- When our sexuality is infused with the Holy Spirit, lovemaking becomes a profoundly mysterious, tender, and generous experience.

WORDS TO REMEMBER

- Let him kiss me with the kisses of his mouth—for your love is more delightful than wine....I belong to my lover and his desire is for me. (Song of Solomon 1:2, 7:10)
- Do not fear, for I am with you; do not look anxiously about you, for I am your God. I will strengthen you, surely I will help you. (Isaiah 41:10, NASB)
- I delight greatly in the LORD; my soul rejoices in my God. For he has clothed me with garments of salvation and arrayed me in a robe of righteousness, as a bridegroom adorns his head like a priest, and as a bride adorns herself with jewels. (Isaiah 61:10)

REAL GUYS

"I really appreciate it when my wife says something nice about me, my job, or my appearance. Hey, I'm 44. It's nice to know my wife appreciates me in my role as husband, father, breadwinner, *and* to know that she still likes how I look."—Chip

PERSONAL REFLECTIONS

1. What is most satisfying to you right now about your sexual intimacy with your husband? What would you like to see improved? Think of three things you can do to create the opportunity for that growth to begin.
2. Complete the following thoughts in your journal:
   Believing that God's design for sexual intimacy is good helps me to understand why...
   Depictions of lovemaking in books and movies have made it easier/more difficult for me to come to terms with...
   Honestly sharing my feelings about my body and sexuality with my husband is...
3. Define in your own words the following terms and concepts used in this chapter:
   ◊ sexual intimacy
   ◊ emotional intimacy
   ◊ romance
   ◊ one-flesh union
   ◊ mutual satisfaction
   ◊ sexual sin
   ◊ transformed by the renewing of your mind
   ◊ conformed to Christ's image
   ◊ body acceptance
   ◊ God's natural design for sexuality

PRAYERS

Praying God's Blessing for Our Marriage

May the Lord make our love increase and overflow for each other and for everyone.... May he strengthen our hearts so that we will be blameless and holy in the presence of our God and Father when our

Lord Jesus comes with all his holy ones.—1 Thessalonians 3:12-13.
Praying God's Blessing for My Husband

And this is my prayer for my husband, Lord: that his love may abound more and more in knowledge and depth of insight, so that he may be able to discern what is best and may be pure and blameless until the day of Christ, filled with the fruit of righteousness that comes through Jesus Christ—to the glory and praise of God.—Philippians 1:9-11

Closing Prayer

O God, our heavenly Father, we know that one of the things that grieves you most is that the most beautiful thing you've given—love—has been so mistreated and so misunderstood in the world.

Lord, help us to understand the sheer perfection of your love in terms of its forgiveness and its sacrifice. Bear down upon our hearts with your Holy Spirit the truth of these things to such a degree that we might have an overwhelming desire to be imitators of God and walk in love, abstaining from its perversions and reproving them on every hand. Make us people who witness to the fact that God is love.

Lord, we have fallen in so many of these areas. Help us to know genuine repentance. Help us to know genuine confession and true cleansing and forgiveness. Lead us on from strength to strength that we might become people who know triumph in previous areas of disaster. It's beautiful to know that in the arms of Jesus and in the fellowship of his church, there is a place for the sinner to come and be cleansed—where they can experience the love of God through loving believers.

Deliver us from the deceptions so prevalent around us. Help us to see right through them and to choose love and to live lives dedicated to you and the coming of your kingdom on earth. In Christ's name. Amen.[4]—Stuart and Jill Briscoe

BLESSINGS NOW

- Welcome your husband in bed: Notice how your body uniquely responds to and communicates with his. Ask him to show you how he likes to be stroked and kissed.
- Create a convivial atmosphere conducive to lovemaking: fresh sheets on the bed, clean surroundings, strategically placed candles, a cool fan on a warm day, your favorite music in the

CD or tape player, and other things that add practical interest and comfort to your love life.

- Whisper in your husband's ear, "Making love with you sounds like a great idea to me tonight."
- Seek God's wisdom and discernment concerning how to respond when you're experiencing difficulty with sexual arousal and responsiveness in your marriage. With the Holy Spirit's help, confront challenging sexual issues and circumstances.
- View lovemaking as a natural extension of your ongoing emotional, physical, and spiritual connection. Nurture your intimate bond with your husband throughout the day via:
  ◊ Frequent eye contact
  ◊ Active listening
  ◊ Mini-massages
  ◊ Holding hands
  ◊ Shared thoughts and feelings
  ◊ Embraces and hugs
  ◊ Intimate gestures
  ◊ Spoken desires
  ◊ Good-bye and hello kisses
  ◊ Mutual prayer
- Make an appointment to make love. Like foreplay, anticipation fuels desire and excitement.
- Minimize interruptions—unplug the phone, resist the urge to talk about unrelated topics, turn off the TV—whether it's for five minutes or five hours. It's okay not to think about anything else other than being with your husband right now.
- Tell your husband something about his body that absolutely, positively delights you.
- Snuggle together as you drift off to sleep after lovemaking. Revel in the gentle gift God has given you to enjoy as a married woman—the matchless feeling of sexual tranquility experienced within the shelter of God's love.

FOR FURTHER READING

Dan B. Allender. *The Wounded Heart*. Colorado Springs: NavPress, 1990.

Stephen Arterburn and Fred Stoeker. *Every Man's Battle: Winning the War on Sexual Temptation One Victory at a Time*. Colorado Springs: WaterBrook, 2000.

Debra Evans. *The Christian Woman's Guide to Sexuality*. Wheaton, Ill.: Crossway, 1997.

Archibald D. Hart. *The Sexual Man*. Nashville: Word, 1995.

Archibald D. Hart, Catherine Hart Weber, and Debra L. Taylor. *Secrets of Eve: Understanding the Mystery of Female Sexuality*. Nashville: Word, 1998.

Donald M. Joy. *Re-bonding: Preventing and Restoring Damaged Relationships*. Waco, Tex.: Word, 1986.

Clifford and Joyce Penner. *52 Ways to Have Fun, Fantastic Sex*. Nashville: Thomas Nelson, 1994.

Clifford and Joyce Penner. *Getting Your Sex Life Off to a Great Start*. Nashville: Thomas Nelson, 1994.

Clifford and Joyce Penner. *A Gift for All Ages*. Waco, Tex.: Word, 1986.

Clifford and Joyce Penner. *The Gift of Sex*. Waco, Tex.: Word, 1981.

Clifford and Joyce Penner. *Restoring the Pleasure*. Waco, Tex.: Word, 1993.

Douglas Rosenau. *A Celebration of Sex: A Guide to Enjoying God's Gift of Sexual Intimacy*. Nashville: Thomas Nelson, 1996.

Lewis Smedes. *Sex for Christians*. Grand Rapids: Eerdmans, 1976.

Lewis Smedes. *Shame and Grace: Healing the Shame We Don't Deserve*. New York: HarperCollins, 1993.

Douglas Weiss. *Intimacy: A 100-Day Guide to Lasting Relationships*. Lake Mary, Fla.: Siloam, 2002.

John White. *Eros Redeemed: Breaking the Stranglehold of Sexual Sin*. Downers Grove, Ill.: InterVarsity, 1993.

Evelyn Eaton Whitehead and James D. Whitehead. *A Sense of Sexuality: Christian Love and Intimacy*. New York: Doubleday, 1980.

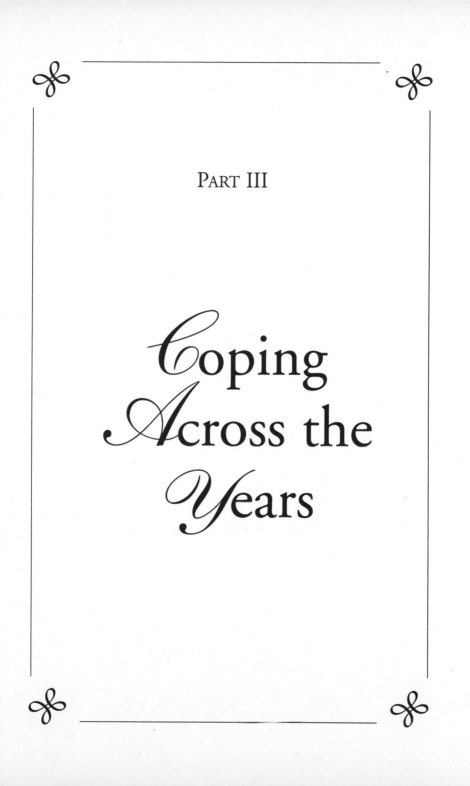

PART III

Coping Across the Years

TEN

*C*risis and *C*ommitment

❦

Believe God's Word and power more than you believe
your own feelings and experiences. Your Rock is Christ,
and it isn't that Rock that ebbs and flows—but your sea.
SAMUEL RUTHERFORD

*A*manda and Jason's wedding day had been like a dream come true. Among the friends and family attending the couple's nuptials, many later said the ceremony was the most beautiful they had ever seen.

The long months of planning and preparing for the farmhouse ceremony resulted in a breathtaking sight not even the best wedding planner could have created: Just as the bride stepped through a vine-covered arbor, the clouds hovering overhead parted, causing the sun to shine down on her face with the warmth of a soft golden spotlight.

Jason's gaze remained fixed on his wife-to-be as she slowly walked forward to join him in marriage. This was the moment Amanda had dreamed about since she was a little girl—and what a beautiful dream it was, set in cultured pearls and a sprinkling of pink powder, trimmed with delicate Belgian lace and yards of white silk, covered in the cool relief of a Maine summer's evening....

During the first year of her marriage, Amanda's thoughts often lingered on her wedding day memories. Upon returning home from their honeymoon, she wondered when her husband would resume the affectionate kissing and cuddling they regularly enjoyed before their marriage. Daily confronting their conflicting desires, real-life sexual scenarios, and the regularity of Jason's persistent requests quickly tempered Amanda's previous view of lovemaking.

Jason wasn't as easy to live with as Amanda thought he would be. Within twelve months, they moved twice. Jason resigned from three jobs before enrolling in a college program for a second degree, then he withdrew from his classes after four weeks.

Late one night, shortly after their first anniversary, Jason told Amanda that what he really wanted to do was form an alternative Christian band that would start practicing in a friend's garage several nights each week. As if this weren't enough to talk about for one evening, within minutes Jason also told Amanda he was considering becoming a pilot, buying an airplane, and earning his income by giving chartered sightseeing tours along the East Coast.

Amanda couldn't believe her ears. Hearing Jason say what he wanted to do next was play guitar professionally, cut a CD, spend their savings on flight school, and invest in a business they had never talked about was just too much. Though she had willingly supported Jason's vocational pursuits, once added to her accumulated concerns, this list of revelations capsized Amanda's coping abilities.

"You know you can do whatever you want, Jason, and I won't stop you," Amanda told her husband, almost in a whisper. "If this is what you want to do with your life, fine, go ahead and do it. But, honey, I've got to confess that right now I'm wondering why I'm still here. As I sit here considering what you say you want to 'do next' with your life, regardless of how I may feel about it or how many times I've heard you say this during the past year," she added quietly, "I realize you're not the man I thought you were when we got married."

Then Amanda spoke the words she thought she would never say to her husband:

"I really don't think I can take any more of this, Jason. Maybe we should get a divorce."

Something Deeper

You're not the man I thought you were.
I really don't think I can take any more of this.
Maybe we should get a divorce.

For many of us, these words are not altogether unfamiliar. Like Amanda, I am certainly no stranger to such "Where do we go from here?" conversations. More than once, I have thought or said, "I really don't think I can take any more of this." And I've also heard my husband make similar remarks to me.

My guess is that you, too, know what it feels like to reach your stress limit. To sometimes wonder how you will keep going for one more day. To now and then long for *something deeper*—the perfect love that "*always* protects, *always* trusts, *always* hopes, *always* perseveres." To every so often think or say, in spite of your best intentions, "I really don't think I can take this any more," or, "Maybe we should get a divorce."

These stunning statements slide into our brain as a first line of defense, don't they? "Sorry," we may say abruptly, almost without thinking; then the word *but* is thrown in as a type of verbal shorthand for "I've reached my limit. I'm finished trying. I've gone as far as I can go." Yet this isn't where we start from in marriage, nor is it the destination we're aiming for.

If a foolproof formula existed this side of heaven for discovering and understanding in each situation the "something deeper" at the heart of every Christian marriage, there would be no reason for me to write this book! You and I both know no such formula exists. Growing in God's wisdom and grace requires the Holy Spirit's slow but steady work within us. As we are little by little conformed to Christ's image and character, countless facets of our just-below-the-surface self will, eventually, rise up and be revealed not only to us, but also to our spouse.

Expect the rough terrain. Our marriage journey involves traveling together through unavoidably rugged territory, no exceptions. "Because perseverance is so difficult," wrote E. B. Pusey, "even when supported by the grace of God, thence is the value of new beginnings.

For new beginnings are the life of perseverance." Remembering this will bring real hope during those dark moments where we discover the way ahead obscured by disappointment, heartache, or doubt. Your new beginning with your husband will come.

Over the years, I've often wept as I've listened to, counseled, and prayed with women facing a marriage crisis. I've learned it's best to react with neither surprise nor shock to the hard things that can happen within anyone's marriage, including my own. I've come to better understand that it's precisely when the hardest things happen to us that we have the greatest opportunity to grow in our relationship with God, draw closer to Christ, and better understand what it means to love the Lord—and our husband. More than ever, I believe the practice of blessing our husband dynamically assists us in fulfilling this holy vow—"to have and to hold from this day forward, for better or worse, for richer for poorer, in sickness and in health, till death us do part, according to God's holy ordinance"—no matter what today's circumstances may be.

By drawing upon our Savior's limitless strength rather than depending upon our own sparse resources, we are ever more encouraged to place our trust in God as He tenderly shapes, directs, and protects our heart, making us the woman, and wife, that He wants us to be.

You're not the man I thought you were....

Do these words convey to you advance warning of a dead end? Or can you see in this familiar phrase a wider avenue for God's blessing?

Along the same route where despair, disillusionment, and defeat may threaten to destroy your marriage, open your eyes. Go deeper. Look straight ahead. I believe you will see God patiently waiting to meet you there.

Life-Changing Choices

A favorite coffee mug sitting on my desk says it well. "DON'T LOOK BACK," reads the caption illustrated by artist Mary Englebreit. A signpost firmly planted at the proverbial fork in the road offers two possible paths: YOUR LIFE to the left and, to the right, NO LONGER AN

OPTION. A confident-looking girl wearing a straw hat marches down the left path in her sagely chosen direction.

This bright picture portrays an apt description of the meaning of the word *crisis*: It's an unexpected fork lying in the middle of your path, "a time," according to my *American Heritage Dictionary*, "when something very important for the future happens or is decided."

Within marriage, some life-changing choices—such as having a child, buying a home, or moving to a new location—can be wonderfully positive experiences. Still others, when all is said and done, are not nearly as big a deal as we initially thought they were, later causing us to wonder why we invested so much time, worry, and anxiety in something we should have known wouldn't qualify as a blip on the life-crisis radar screen.

Then there are the hard things—those heartbreaking marital circumstances so stunning in scale that when they appear on the horizon you feel as if you have reached the end of your ability to cope. We know the list of possibilities is long because we have walked with our mother and sisters, daughters and friends, neighbors and relatives as they have confronted family crises. Many of us have reached the fork in the road ourself.

Cheryl's crisis appeared when she and her husband, Don, moved from their nine-year home in Rochester, Michigan, to Phoenix, where Don's new job offered him a significant promotion. Together, the couple felt grateful for the opportunity to enter the next phase of marriage with an enlarged horizon for ministry, and Don was especially looking forward to the job challenges ahead. After their move west, however, something entirely unexpected happened. About this experience, Cheryl later wrote:

> It's as if a stranger appeared in Don's place on the day we
> reached Arizona, and the man I'd intimately known for more
> than two decades decided to take a temporary leave of absence
> from our marriage. Even when physically present, Don's heart
> and mind seemed far away; he was no longer "with" us, and the
> husband and dad we previously knew didn't return to us until
> he resigned from his job.

First, I experienced a full-blown case of shock, denial, and disbelief. Then I went into an extended period of mourning, learning to trust God in ways never required before. Looking back from today's vantage point, I recognize the dramatic growth God promoted in our marriage, and in us, starting with our first night in Arizona. Thanks to His goodness and grace, our marriage didn't just survive Don's tenure in Phoenix—eventually, we thrived.

During those three seemingly interminable years, I spent a lot of time each day praying, often wondering: *Will our bond weather the storm?* Over the course of our extended growing season, I honestly didn't know how things would turn out. For a long time, what I really wanted was for God to change my husband in the ways *I* thought he needed changing. I wanted *control*. Instead, I found myself firmly placed in a position where God turned off the usual lights, where He faithfully kept me growing in the dark. Without a doubt, God wanted me to put my trust in Him to save my marriage, but the Lover of my soul also wanted something more.

I wish I could tell you I was a quick learner. I wasn't. I would love to be able to share that I easily abandoned my well-meaning but useless attempts to change and control Don's attitudes, lifestyle, and behavior. I can't. Behind closed doors, I cried, I whined, I moped, I moaned. Sometimes my heart hurt with a dull ache I didn't think I could bear another minute. I noticed whenever I tried to help my husband refocus his heart, *I* was the one who felt like a failure, as well as a fool.

Finally, in my utter, flat-on-my-face helplessness, during my quiet time one afternoon, the Lord's dependable love broke through. By God's grace, I gave up trying to turn Don's heart back toward home, acknowledging that I couldn't change, control, or heal my husband's innermost being. At that point, my primary prayer changed from, "Lord, save my husband from the snares of death so that he might return to me," to "Lord, bless my husband so that he may become the man You created him to be." With the Lord's strong help and the Holy Spirit's steadfast direction, I accepted my own heart's acute need. I saw that *only by placing Jesus Christ first in my heart could I become the loving wife God desired me to be.* As I more closely considered God's Word and waited in Christ's presence, I understood the central challenge—and opportunity—of our marriage crisis, realizing in which way I needed to go: *Love the Lord your God with all your heart and with all your soul and with all your mind. This is the first and greatest commandment* (Matthew 22:37).

I thought: How can I love God above everyone and everything else when I place my desire to love and be loved by my husband above my desire to love and be loved by God? If my need for Don's affirmation and approval was overdominating my heart's affections, then not only did I not know and love the Lord the way I thought I did—I also didn't love my husband the way God wanted me to.

Forget all those silly love songs. This was the real deal. It was so good to more fully know that Jesus' love is the perfect, never-ending love my heart longs for; that no matter what happens, He will never leave me or forsake me; that with Him alone do I have the unfailing forever-yours romance I've dreamed of my entire life—love's perfect reality beyond today's shadowy reflection, pointing toward the glorious marriage that will one day come to pass in heaven when we shall behold him "face to face" (1 Corinthians 13:12).

That's when I really, truly, and deeply knew: My husband was in good hands, and so was I. Coming to grips with the reality of my need to let go of Don and trust God more completely has since allowed me to view our marriage, my love for my husband, and my love for the Lord in a whole new way.

Twentieth-century evangelist Oswald Chambers wrote: "One of the severest lessons comes from the stubborn refusal to see that we must not interfere in other people's lives. It takes a long time to realize the danger of being an amateur providence, that is, interfering with God's order for others. You see a certain person suffering, and you say—He shall not suffer, and I will see that he does not. You put your hand straight in front of God's permissive will to prevent it, and God says—'What is it to thee?'"

Chambers adds: "If there is stagnation spiritually, never allow it to go on, but get into God's presence and find out the reason for it. Possibly you will find it is because you have been interfering in the life of another; proposing things you had no right to propose; advising when you had no right to advise. When you do have to give advice to another, God will advise through you with the direct understanding of His Spirit; your part is to be so rightly related to God that His discernment comes through you all the time for the blessing of another soul."[1]

Open Your Eyes

Open your eyes to signs of the unhealthy in yourself, your husband, your marriage, and have the courage to admit any problems that may be there. God is the Master at helping His children work out their troubles, but not if they pretend that problems don't exist. Profound, lasting change comes to those who face their problems with God's help and take action!

I also encourage you to team up with other women for prayer and encouragement. It's the isolated woman who is most at risk for enabling behavior. A group of other women can help you "define reality" by offering objectivity and perspective.

Some wives are up against forces that require more serious, and even professional, help. You should seek that help if any of the following conditions apply to your marriage:

- If there is physical abuse of any kind, either by you or your husband, toward any member of the family.
- If you are afraid to speak your own mind or express your feelings.
- If you take responsibility for your husband's behavior or his feelings (for example, if you blame yourself when he gets angry).
- If you make excuses or "cover" for your husband's behavior (for example, if you call in sick for him when he is hung over).

Get Help When You Need It

When facing intense marital conflict, it's only natural for us to want to be an "amateur providence" as we initially lose our bearings, become disoriented, blame our spouse, feel substantial self-pity, withdraw emotionally and physically, and discover we want to give up, among other things. Nevertheless, it's precisely at each critical juncture of extraordinary importance that we most need to take a step of faith and make a courageous choice—a determined resolution to rely upon God's Word, the Holy Spirit's help, and the sound counsel of mature Christian advisors.

- If there is any sexual infidelity, aberration, or manipulation.
- If you feel guilt or shame over the way your husband treats you.
- If there are addictions or substance abuses of any kind (for example, alcohol, drugs, pornography, sex, gambling, even work).
- If there is chronic debt, chronic unemployment, or frequent changes from job to job.
- If there are constant, chronic arguments and conflict.
- If weeks or months go by without serious, heart-to-heart talks between you and your husband concerning any serious problems you believe are present in your relationship.

Where can you turn for help? That depends on the nature and extent of the problem.... A minister, priest, or doctor may be able to point you in the right direction. Many churches have special programs addressing some of the needs mentioned in the list above.

Wives, be on your guard against enabling your husband to "get away" with irresponsible, abusive behaviors. God calls you to be his "helper," but helper doesn't mean enabler. So, don't be! Even if your man resists making changes, take responsibility for yourself and look for help. Do it now! God doesn't ask you to suffer in silence, especially when He has provided so many resources to help you in your distress.[2]—Robert Lewis and William Hendricks

⚘ ⚘ ⚘

When the storm hits, it's not unusual for one partner to avoid seeking outside help when lacking the other spouse's knowledge or approval. Since each partner plays an equal part in creating the total marriage experience, however, we wives must take responsibility for our share of the relationship; we must not neglect seeking marriage-saving aid in favor of "not rocking the boat."

"Certainly, a wife needs to pray, but she also needs to act. In seeking help, some women actually begin to be a real help to their husbands for the first time," confirm pastors Robert Lewis and William Hendricks. "Don't be afraid to get more than one opinion about the nature of your problem and the course of action you should take. 'In abundance of counselors there is victory' (Proverbs 11:14). This also provides much needed security and reassurance when contemplating tough steps of action!"[3]

If we sincerely desire our marriage to be strong and healthy, we must begin, with God's help, to become healthier ourself. If we ask Him for clear direction, as Cheryl did, the Lord will show us *specifically* where and how we need to change. This restorative process requires taking a fearless moral inventory of our life, starting with these poignant verses from Psalm 139:

Search me, O God, and know my heart;
Try me and know my anxious thoughts;
And see if there be any hurtful way in me,
And lead me in the everlasting way. (Psalm 139:23-24, NASB)

Our moral inventory, if we're completely honest, will take some time to complete. Praying the last two verses of Psalm 139 with any real sincerity results in an "ouch!" unlike any other we experience. But, in this way, with the aid of much prayer, Bible study, pastoral care, and good counsel from not only church staff but also from caring Christian friends, our focus turns from feelings of loss, anger, disappointment, failure, and blame toward God's curative treatment of our fears. As we lay our heart's burdens down, one by one, at the foot of the cross, we receive our heavenly Father's gift of peace.

To better understand the "what, why, and how" of our part in a marital crisis or conflict, we greatly benefit from asking God to "Search...try...know...see...and lead" us as we daily walk with Him—not that He doesn't already know us through and through, for we also read in Psalm 139:1-6:

> O LORD, you have searched me and you know me. You know when I sit and when I rise; you perceive my thoughts from afar. You discern my going out and my lying down; you are familiar with all my ways. Before a word is on my tongue you know it completely, O LORD. You hem me in—behind and before; you have laid your hand upon me. Such knowledge is too wonderful for me, too lofty for me to attain.

The point, I believe, is that we need to *ask*—we need to answer the Lord's persistent knocking on the door of our heart, let Him in, and give Him permission to perform this particular work within us.

Knowing our limitations also includes acknowledging the value of seeking professional and/or pastoral assistance when depression, a drug or alcohol habit, sexual aberration, or any other serious concern becomes evident. Getting the help we need shows our husband that we're willing to stand by him during tough times, that we cherish him enough to honestly face his pain, that we aren't afraid to take responsibility for our part—and that we'll leave his share of the responsibility for making necessary changes with him.

Learning to depend on God during life's difficult crises comes when we're willing to risk growing in the dark. God's unfailing love often is most powerfully revealed to us as we meet Him in the midst of our broken, bulldozed, bottomed-out places, for that's when we're more apt to call upon the Lord with our whole heart, depend more deeply on His grace, and recognize we've been drawn into God's divine embrace—the sustaining intimacy of a holy relationship with our risen Savior.

FOCUS POINTS

- The marriage journey involves traveling together through unavoidably rugged territory. Remembering that "new beginnings are the life of perseverance" brings real hope during those dark moments where we discover the way ahead obscured by disappointment, heartache, or doubt.

- Growing in God's wisdom and grace requires the Holy Spirit's slow but steady work within us. As we are little by little conformed to Christ's image and character, countless facets of our just-below-the-surface self will, eventually, rise up and be revealed not only to us, but also to our spouse.

- It's precisely when the hardest things happen to us that we have the greatest opportunity to grow in our relationship with God, draw closer to Christ, and better understand what it means to love the Lord—and our husband. The practice of blessing our husband dynamically assists us in fulfilling our vows, no matter what today's circumstances may be.

- When facing intense marital conflict, it's natural for us to want to be an "amateur providence." Nevertheless, this is when we most need to take a step of faith and make a courageous choice—a determined resolution to rely upon God's Word, the Holy Spirit's help, and the sound counsel of mature Christian advisors.

WORDS TO REMEMBER

- Blessed is he whose help is the God of Jacob, whose hope is in the LORD his God. (Psalm 146:5)

- May my cry come before you, O LORD; give me understanding according to your word. May my supplication come before you; deliver me according to your promise. (Psalm 119:169-170)

- In this world you will have trouble. But take heart! I have overcome the world. (John 16:33)

- Let us hold unswervingly to the hope we profess, for he who promised is faithful. (Hebrews 10:23)

- Let your eyes look straight ahead, fix your gaze directly before you. Make level paths for your feet and take only ways that are firm. Do not swerve to the right or the left; keep your foot from evil. (Proverbs 4:25-27)

REAL GUYS

"When she doesn't agree with me, my wife will always let me know about it in her no-nonsense way. Of course, I don't always appreciate it, but knowing I'll always get it straight up from her is a huge blessing."—Adam

PERSONAL REFLECTIONS

1. If you're facing a difficult passage in your marriage, take time now to pray and seek God's wisdom in His Word. Ask Him to direct your steps. Spend time listening to His still, small voice. In your journal, express what's on your heart and what you've just learned by reading the Scriptures.

2. Complete these thoughts in your journal:
   At this time in my life the most challenging areas in my marriage to surrender to Christ's lordship are...
   When I feel discouraged or disheartened about my marriage, God comforts me by...
   The Lord's love has broken through in my marriage most clearly when...

3. Reflect on the ways God has used you to uniquely express His love to your husband during a difficult time in your mate's life. Write in your journal about what the experience was like for the two of you, paying special attention to what you saw in your marriage and yourself as a result of being in this situation. How might the positive elements of those events and your response to them apply to your circumstances today?

PRAYERS

Praying God's Blessing for Our Marriage

May the Lord answer us when we are in distress; may the name of the God of Jacob protect us. May he send us help from the sanctuary and grant us support from Zion. May he remember all our sacrifices and accept our burnt offerings. May he give us the desire of our hearts and make all our plans succeed. We will shout for joy when we are victorious and will lift up our banners in the name of our God. May the Lord grant all our requests.—Psalm 20:1-5

Praying God's Blessing for My Husband
    May my husband's eyes look straight ahead, may he fix his gaze directly before him. May he make level paths for his feet and take only ways that are firm. May he not swerve to the right or the left; may he keep his foot from evil.—Proverbs 4:25-27

Closing Prayer
    O Almighty God, help us to put away all bitterness and wrath and evil-speaking, with all malice. May we possess our souls in patience, however we are tempted and provoked, and not be overcome with evil, but overcome evil with good. Enable, O God of patience, to bear one another's burdens, and to forbear one another with love. Oh, teach and help us all to live in peace and to love in truth, following peace with all people and walking in love, as Christ loved us, of whom let us learn such meekness and lowliness of heart that in Him we may find rest for our souls. Subdue all bitter resentments in our minds, and let the law of kindness be on our tongues, and a meek and quiet spirit in all our lives. Make us so gentle and peaceable that we may be followers of Thee as dear children, that Thou, the God of peace, mayest dwell with us evermore. Amen.[4]—Benjamin Jenks (1646-1724)

BLESSINGS NOW

- Cling to the Rock when hard things happen in your marriage. Run, don't walk, to your tower of safety: Jesus Christ. Your heart is forever safe in His hands.
- Pray for your husband. Then pray some more. And keep on praying. (See chapter 11.)
- Wrap up your concerns, worries, and doubts about your marriage; firmly place this heavy parcel under the cross. Linger long enough to surrender your desire for control of the situation—that is, until you're willing to fully set your burden down, let go, and leave it behind you at the feet of Christ.
- Believe God's enduring promises apply at all times, in every situation. Through thick and thin, count on this truth: "And we know that in all things God works for the good of those who love him, who have been called according to his purpose" (Romans 8:28).

- Grieve as necessary. Gain emotional stability by honestly facing and dealing with your pain, shock, and/or anguish. Get help when you need additional Christ-centered support and perspective, even if your husband won't get help with you.
- Realize the danger of being an "amateur providence" for your husband. Draw close to the Lord before giving your spouse advice. Seek God's wisdom and understanding; pray for His discernment, that your words may be a blessing rather than a burden to your husband.
- Feast at the Lord's banquet table when you feel inwardly hungry and depleted. Gain vital spiritual nourishment through:
  ◊ regular Bible reading and study.
  ◊ the Holy Spirit's infilling, intercession, and guidance.
  ◊ private prayer and worship.
  ◊ quiet reflection on the Psalms.
  ◊ counsel and mentoring from mature believers.
  ◊ obedience by faith to God's commands.
- Meet your basic needs for sleep, healthful food, and exercise. If you discover yourself lapsing into unhealthy lifestyle patterns, make an appointment with your primary care provider to discuss positive self-care strategies. (See chapter 6.)
- Meditate on the Word so that you will not grow weary and lose heart: Fix your eyes on your Lord and Savior, the author and finisher of your faith (Hebrews 12:2-4).
- Ask God to give you grace to persevere. Place your hope in Him alone—the mighty King who can move mountains. Whatever the problem or crisis, God is bigger: He reigns above and beyond your current circumstances.

FOR FURTHER READING

Jerry Bridges. *Trusting God.* Colorado Springs: NavPress, 1988.

Jill Briscoe. *Out of the Storm and into God's Arms: Shelter in Turbulent Times.* Colorado Springs: Shaw/WaterBrook, 2000.

Timothy Clinton. *Before a Bad Goodbye.* Nashville: Word, 1999.

Henry Cloud and John Townsend. *How People Grow: What the Bible Reveals about Personal Growth.* Grand Rapids: Zondervan, 2002.

Larry Crabb. *Shattered Dreams: God's Unexpected Pathway to Joy.*
  Colorado Springs: WaterBrook, 2001.
James Dobson. *When God Doesn't Make Sense.* Wheaton, Ill.:
  Tyndale, 1993.
Billy Graham. *Hope for the Troubled Heart: Finding God in the Midst
  of Pain.* Nashville: Word/Thomas Nelson, 1991.
D. Martyn Lloyd-Jones. *The Cross.* Christopher Catherwood, ed.
  Wheaton, Ill.: Crossway, 1986.
Michael J. McManus, *Marriage Savers.* Grand Rapids: Zondervan,
  1993.
J. Keith Miller. *A Hunger for Healing: The Twelve Steps as a Classic
  Model for Christian Spiritual Growth.* San Francisco: HarperSan-
  Francisco, 1991.
Henri J. M. Nouwen. *Turn My Mourning into Dancing: Moving
  Through Hard Times with Hope.* Compiled and edited by
  Timothy Jones. Nashville: Word, 2001.
Les and Leslie Parrott. *Saving Your Marriage Before It Starts: Seven
  Questions to Ask Before (and After) You Marry.* Grand Rapids:
  Zondervan, 1995.
Edith Schaeffer. *Affliction.* Old Tappan, N.J.: Fleming H. Revell,
  1978.
Scott Stanley, Daniel Trathen, Savanna McCain, and Milt Bryan. *A
  Lasting Promise: A Christian Guide to Fighting for Your Marriage.*
  San Francisco: Jossey-Bass, 1998.
Sheldon Vanauken. *A Severe Mercy.* San Francisco: Harper & Row,
  1977.

ELEVEN

Prayer and Patience

❧

Real prayer comes not from gritting our teeth,
but from falling in love.
RICHARD FOSTER

One thing that has really amazed me at various turning points in my marriage is this: When I should have been the most afraid, God supplied vigorous courage. When I should have been completely confused, God provided holy wisdom. When I should have been totally exhausted, God sent life-giving strength.

This doesn't mean, of course, that I've never been afraid, confused, or exhausted—far from it! As a woman and a wife, I'm well acquainted with my manifold weaknesses. On the other hand, I also know the mysterious power that can arrive, without warning, at precisely the moment I least expect it—the wonder of constantly being cared for and guarded by a compassionate Father whose plans and purposes for His beloved children can't be thwarted.

Since our testiest spiritual struggles in this respect often take place inside the stress-filled territory of marital crisis—family upheaval, the loss of a job, or a husband's struggle with pornography, for example— it's not difficult to lose our bearings. We may sometimes forget our best weapons against the enemy's attacks don't require us to muster superhuman strength to use them effectively.

"Be strong in the Lord and in *his* mighty power," declared the apostle Paul. "Put on the full armor of God so that you can take your stand against the devil's schemes" (Ephesians 6:10-11; emphasis added) —a lasting insight we're more likely to acquire during one of life's trials and from then on recall the scope of the struggle. Paul continues in verses 12-18:

> For our struggle is not against flesh and blood, but against the rulers, against the authorities, against the powers of this dark world and against the spiritual forces of evil in the heavenly realms. Therefore put on the full armor of God, so that when the day of evil comes, you may be able to stand your ground, and after you have done everything, to stand. Stand firm then, with the belt of truth buckled around your waist, with the breastplate of righteousness in place, and with your feet fitted with the readiness that comes from the gospel of peace. In addition to all this, take up the shield of faith, with which you can extinguish all the flaming arrows of the evil one. Take the helmet of salvation and the sword of the Spirit, which is the word of God. And pray in the Spirit on all occasions with all kinds of prayers and requests. With this in mind, be alert and always keep on praying for all the saints.

While it's vital to put on God's armor every morning as soon as we wake and to "Always keep on praying," we do well to also keep this in mind: *The battle belongs to the Lord.* God does the fighting in the heavenly realms *for* us. Brought to the limit of our coping ability, we discover why we must surrender and stand firm simultaneously.

Prayer Is the Greater Work

As we grow in the experience of blessing our husband, we increasingly learn that prayer accomplishes the impossible on our behalf: What we can't do in and for our marriage, God *can* do.

Persistently interceding for our husband in prayer is a distinctly Christian privilege, a responsibility that bears fruit in season, producing a timely harvest that benefits our family, our community, our church, and our nation for generations to come. "Prayer does not fit us for the greater works; prayer *is* the greater work," Oswald Chambers reminds us.[1] In practical terms, this means making prayer a top priority in our relationship with our husband.

Through prayer, we can see who's *really* in control as we purposely lay our burdens at Christ's feet, one by one. Without a doubt, prayer is a wife's best defense against the enemy's schemes. Prayer is also the safe place we retreat to when we need to receive patience, accept our limitations, and ask for steady help, sustenance, and direction, especially when our influence approaches its limit.

"Our first prayer needs simply to tell God, 'Oh God, help me to pray, because I cannot pray by myself,'" Dr. James Houston declares in *The Transforming Power of Prayer.* "Such a prayer helps us to recognize how prayer expresses our deepest need before the kingship of God."[2]

When marriage brings us to the end of ourself, when we know beyond a shadow of a doubt that we cannot conjure up peace and patience independent from the Holy Spirit's gifting, when our heart cries out for rest and strength in the midst of our daily life as it is actually lived moment by moment, Jesus stands at the door and knocks. "Come unto me," He says, as only our Good Shepherd can—and prayer is where we meet Him.

Prayer is the place we take the loads that weigh heavy on our heart, leaving them at the foot of the cross. In prayer, we turn to face God as we are, with longing and hunger and thirst, asking to be filled again. Prayer is the entry point into the practice of patience, the means by which we surrender our burdens, accept our limitations, see the next step, and receive spiritual endurance to stand firm in God's strength rather than our own.

"Aspire to God with short but frequent outpourings of the heart; admire His bounty; invoke His aid; cast yourself in spirit at the foot of the cross; adore His goodness; treat with Him of your salvation; give Him your whole soul a thousand times a day," the fifteenth-century spiritual director Frances de Sales advised.[3] This is an outstanding summary of our much-needed marital prayer plan, don't you think?

I realize that this probably sounds familiar. More than likely, you've already spent uncounted hours praying for your husband.

When we know that we have no real ability to control a particular problem or situation, prayer becomes our most important action. Here's a quick scriptural summary of why—and how—prayer works on our behalf in this regard:

- *Prayer recognizes who is in control:* "I call on you, O God, for you will answer me; give ear to me and hear my prayer" (Psalm 17:6).

- *Prayer builds the spiritual strength of Christ's followers:* "…we have not stopped praying for you and asking God to fill you with the knowledge of his will through all spiritual wisdom and understanding. And we pray this in order that you may live a life worthy of the Lord and may please him in every way: bearing fruit in every good work, growing in the knowledge of God, being strengthened with all power according to his glorious might so that you may have great endurance and patience, and joyfully giving thanks to the Father, who has qualified you to share in the inheritance of the saints in the kingdom of light" (Colossians 1:9-12).

- *Prayer brings protection from harm:* "Therefore let everyone who is godly pray to you while you may be found; surely when the waters rise, they will not reach him" (Psalm 32:6).

- *Prayer lightens the load:* "To the LORD I cry aloud, and he answers me from his holy hill" (Psalm 3:4).

✤ ✤ ✤ ───────────────────────────

Lift Up Your Heart!

Let reason do all that reason can. Employ it as far as it will go. But, at the same time, acknowledge that it is utterly incapable of giving either faith, or hope, or love, and consequently of producing either real virtue or substantial happiness. Expect these from a higher source, even from the Father of the spirits of all flesh. Seek and receive them, not as your own acquisition, but as the gift of God. Lift up your hearts to him who "giveth to all men liberally and upbraideth not."

- *Prayer partners with thanksgiving:* "Be joyful always; pray continually; give thanks in all circumstances, for this is God's will for you in Christ Jesus" (1 Thessalonians 5:16-18).
- *Prayer goes where we cannot go and does what we cannot do:* "We do not know what we ought to pray for, but the Spirit himself intercedes for us with groans that words cannot express. And he who searches our hearts knows the mind of the Spirit, because the Spirit intercedes for the saints in accordance with God's will" (Romans 8:26-27).
- *Prayer defeats the opposition:* "Put on the full armor of God so that you can take your stand against the devil's schemes.... Pray in the Spirit on all occasions with all kinds of prayers and requests. With this in mind, be alert and always keep praying...." (Ephesians 6:11, 18).
- *Prayer provides wisdom:* "If any of you lacks wisdom, he should ask God, who gives generously to all without finding fault, and it will be given to him" (James 1:5).
- *Prayer promotes peace:* "Do not be anxious about anything, but in everything, by prayer and petition, with thanksgiving, present your requests to God. And the peace of God, which transcends all understanding, will guard your hearts and your minds in Christ Jesus" (Philippians 4:6-7).
- *Prayer puts our love for others into action:* "And this is my prayer: that your love may abound more and more in knowledge and

---

He alone can give that faith which is "the evidence" and conviction "of things not seen." He alone can "beget you unto a lively hope" of an inheritance eternal in the heavens; and he alone can "shed his love abroad in your heart by the Holy Ghost given unto you."

Ask, therefore, and it shall be given you! Cry unto him, and you shall not cry in vain! So shall you be living witnesses that wisdom, holiness and happiness are one, inseparably united and are indeed the beginning of that eternal life which God hath given us in his Son.[4]—John Wesley (1703-1791)

✿ ✿ ✿

depth of insight, so that you may be able to discern what is best and may be pure and blameless until the day of Christ, filled with the fruit of righteousness that comes through Jesus Christ—to the glory and praise of God" (Philippians 1:9-11).

Give It Up

Control. It's something every wife at times wishes she could have in reality—especially when circumstances swerve dizzyingly out of reach, breaking through our emotional defenses.

Faced with the frustration of our personal finiteness, we can learn to view our human limitations in a different way: We can see and understand that the control we thought we had over our husband's life was never really control at all. It was influence.

When it comes to our husband, of course we do everything in our power to protect him from hurt and harm. The number of our husband's life events and experiences that we may *influence* but can't ultimately *control*, however, is much larger than we may admit. On days when I'm tempted to forget this fact, I find it helpful to reflect on the following noteworthy list:

Events, Experiences, and Personal Traits That I May Influence—But Can't Control—In My Husband's Life
- his personality and temperament
- his aptitudes, skills, and abilities
- his emotional, social, and spiritual growth
- his health and safety status
- his conversion and devotion to Christ
- his level of career achievement
- his vocational choices
- his financial and social status
- the use of his gifts and talents
- his size, appearance, and fitness level
- his decisions to engage in healthy or unhealthy habits: diet, exercise, smoking, alcohol use, overworking, overspending, and so on
- his passions, preferences, and personal tastes

• his peer-group choices

• his state of happiness and emotional well-being

Instead of seeking control, we can recognize God's handiwork in every moment, at each stage of life, whether it's painful or pleasurable, easy or difficult, frustrating or satisfying. Viewed through this lens, we see our husband's life comprises a much larger, grander landscape than we can possibly see in the shifting patterns of day-to-day circumstances. Though we can't view the entire picture yet, we can rest in the assurance that the Lord faithfully loves our husband and is tenderly working for his good, even in the tiniest details. The sovereign Painter is creating a priceless masterpiece. We can trust Him to complete His job—perfectly.

But, let's be honest: It's so much easier to believe this when things are going smoothly, isn't it? Conflicts can arise that cause us to feel our inadequacies and lack of control as never before. Sometimes, our direct intervention may be needed, taking us into unexplored territory that no longer feels safe to us.

So, when the going gets rough, remember what the wives I've talked to and heard from say has helped them most:

• Read the Psalms.

• Give your concerns to Jesus.

• Do what you can.

• Consider and rely on what the Scriptures say.

• Put God's armor on every morning.

• Get the support you need.

• Place your husband in the Lord's hands.

• Stand firm in Christ's strength.

• Always keep praying.

Isn't it comforting to remember that our heavenly Father has things under control? That His compassionate design for our life and our marriage never wavers? That we can trust the Creator of the universe to accomplish what we can't possibly do for our husband and ourself?

We can count on this: God's love for our husband exceeds our highest expectations, our fondest hopes, our most fervent desires for his good—and no matter what today looks like, we can rest in the knowledge that His purposes for our spouse's life will not fail.

FOCUS POINTS

- Prayer is the entry point into the practice of patience, the means by which we surrender our burdens, accept our limitations, see the next step, and receive spiritual endurance to go on in God's strength rather than our own.
- When we know that we have no real ability to control a particular problem or situation, prayer becomes our most important means of action.
- As we grow in the experience of blessing our husband, we increasingly learn that prayer accomplishes the things that we cannot carry out in ourselves—or in others.
- Through prayer, we find the strength to be quiet as we wait for the answers only God can give.

WORDS TO REMEMBER

- The eyes of the LORD are on the righteous and his ears are attentive to their cry.... The righteous cry out, and the LORD hears them; he delivers them from all their troubles. The LORD is close to the brokenhearted and saves those who are crushed in spirit. (Psalm 34:15, 17-18)
- You are forgiving and good, O LORD, abounding in love to all who call to you. Hear my prayer, O LORD; listen to my cry for mercy. In the day of my trouble I will call to you, for you will answer me. (Psalm 86:5-7)
- Ask and it will be given to you; seek and you will find; knock and the door will be opened to you. For everyone who asks receives; he who seeks finds; and to him who knocks, the door will be opened. (Matthew 7:7-8)
- In the morning, O LORD, you hear my voice; in the morning I lay my requests before you and wait in expectation. (Psalm 5:3)

REAL GUYS

"No matter how bad my wife's day was, she always takes the time to sit and ask me how my day was. She listens with love and compassion. Then we pray together, which tremendously helps me to lift the weight of the day's problems off my shoulders and reassures me that God's will prevails."—Bill

PERSONAL REFLECTIONS

1. After reading this chapter and considering God's Word, ask the Lord what changes, if any, He would like you to make regarding your prayers for your husband. Record your thoughts and reflections about this vitally important marital responsibility. When you have finished, spend some time praying for your husband.
2. Complete these thoughts in your journal:
   At this time in my life the most challenging areas in my marriage to surrender to Christ's lordship are…
   When I feel concerned about my husband, prayer provides…
   Praying for my husband encourages me to remember…
3. Make a list of some things you can do to ensure that praying for your marriage becomes a daily habit and not only a crisis response.

PRAYERS

Praying God's Blessing for Our Marriage

Lord, make all grace abound to us, for you are able, so that in all things at all times, having all that we need, we may abound in every good work. 2 Corinthians 9:8

Praying God's Blessing for My Husband

I pray my husband will trust in you today with his whole heart, Father, and lean not on his own understanding; may he acknowledge you in all his ways, that you will make his paths straight.—Proverbs 3:5-6

Closing Prayer

Hear our prayers, O Lord, and consider our desires. Give unto us true humility, a meek and quiet spirit, a loving and a friendly demeanor, a holy and a useful manner of life; bearing the burdens of our neighbors, denying ourselves, and studying to benefit others, and to please Thee in all things. Grant us to be righteous in performing promises, loving to our relatives, careful of our charges; to be gentle and easy to be entreated, slow to anger, and readily prepared for every good work. Amen.[5]—Jeremy Taylor (1613-1667)

BLESSINGS NOW

- Cry out to God for help, and rest in His sovereign ability and reap the supernatural results. Trust God's power, rule, and authority. His design and purposes for your life and for your husband's life will not fail.
- Ask God to make a way for you and your husband to pray together regularly if you don't already. Also ask God to direct you to a godly woman who will partner with you in prayer for your marriage: "Again, I tell you that if two of you on earth agree about anything you ask for, it will be done for you by my Father in heaven" (Matthew 18:19).
- Turn to the Psalms and pray them aloud as you cope with your fears, express your doubts, give voice to your heart's deepest desires, and praise God for His unfailing promises.
- Hand over your past and present failures to God. Ask Him to lead you step by step into the future, believing He will bless your ministry to your husband for His glory. Remember that "the one who calls you is faithful" (1 Thessalonians 5:24), and He will take care of you.
- Grow in the fertile ground of your marital stresses and strains, even in the dark. Coming to terms with your weaknesses and facing your failures isn't a painless process, but can be very healing.
- Write down your unresolved conflicts, feelings, fears, and thoughts concerning your husband and your marriage. Going through the list, pray about each item.
- Stand firm; be courageous! If you have not yet done so, memorize Ephesians 6:14-18. Put God's armor on first thing every morning, one piece at a time.
- Recognize the vital difference between influence and control. Seek God's wisdom as you daily discover new ways to rely upon His perfect strengh in your weakness.

FOR FURTHER READING

Neil T. Anderson. *The Bondage Breaker.* Eugene, Ore.: Harvest House, 1990.

Kay Arthur. *Lord, Is It Warfare? Teach Me to Stand.* Colorado Springs: WaterBrook, 2001.

E. M. Bounds. *The Necessity of Prayer.* Grand Rapids: Baker, 1976.

Jerry Bridges. *How to Get Results Through Prayer.* Colorado Springs: NavPress, 1975.

Jill Briscoe. *Prayer That Works.* Wheaton, Ill.: Tyndale, 2000.

Oswald Chambers. *Prayer: A Holy Occupation.* Grand Rapids: Discovery House, 1992.

Evelyn Christenson. *What Happens When We Pray for Our Families.* Wheaton, Ill.: Victor, 1992.

Richard J. Foster. *Prayer: Finding the Heart's True Home.* San Francisco: HarperSanFrancisco, 1992.

S. D. Gordon. *Quiet Talks on Prayer.* Westwood, N.J.: The Christian Library, 1984.

James Houston. *The Transforming Power of Prayer.* Colorado Springs: NavPress, 1996.

Jan Johnson. *When the Soul Listens: Finding Rest and Direction in Contemplative Prayer.* Colorado Springs: NavPress, 1999.

C. S. Lewis. *Letters to Malcolm: Chiefly on Prayer.* New York: Harvest/Harcourt Brace Jovanovich, 1964.

C. S. Lewis. *The Screwtape Letters.* New York: Macmillan, 1948.

Calvin Miller. *Disarming the Darkness: A Guide to Spiritual Warfare.* Grand Rapids: Zondervan, 1998.

Beth Moore. *Praying God's Word: Breaking Free from Spiritual Strongholds.* Nashville: Broadman & Holman, 2000.

Henri J. M. Nouwen. *The Only Necessary Thing: Living a Prayerful Life.* Wendy Wilson Greer, ed. New York: Crossroad, 1999.

The One Year Book of Personal Prayer. Wheaton, Ill.: Tyndale, 1991.

Les Parrott. *The Control Freak: Coping with Those Around You, Taming the One Within.* Wheaton, Ill.: Tyndale, 2000.

Eugene H. Peterson. *Answering God: The Psalms As Tools for Prayer.* San Francisco: HarperSanFrancisco, 1989.

Eugene H. Peterson. *Praying with Jesus: A Year of Daily Prayer and Reflections on the Words and Actions of Jesus.* San Francisco: HarperSanFrancisco, 1993.

A. W. Tozer. *Spiritual Warfare.* Camp Hill, Penn.: Christian Publications, 1996.

TWELVE

The Unbreakable Three-Strand Cord

❧

Two are better than one, because they have a good return for
their work: If one falls down, his friend can help him up.
But pity the man who falls and has no one to help him up!
Also, if two lie down together, they will keep warm.
But how can one keep warm alone? Though one may
be overpowered, two can defend themselves.
A cord of three strands is not quickly broken.
ECCLESIASTES 4:9-12

*J*esus is actively at work at the center of our marriage—the third
strand of the well-weathered cord that cannot be easily broken.
His plans and purposes for us are for our good.

As we walk side by side with our husband toward eternity and our
time with him unfolds, our sacred bond is continually renewed
though loving God: The love we share together arises from the rich
reservoir of God's unfailing faithfulness, mercy, and grace toward us—
the basis of our present joy and future hope.

"A Christian marriage is a commitment involving three individuals—husband, wife, and Jesus Christ," asserts noted marriage and
family counselor Dr. H. Norman Wright. "It is a pledge of mutual

fidelity and submission. Marriage is also one of God's greatest schools of learning, for it can be a place where a husband and wife are refined. The rough edges are gradually filed away until there is a greater and smoother working and blending together, and both individuals are fulfilled."[1]

On the surface, it's easy to be fooled into thinking our needs and expectations can be met by the man we married. But the marriage journey involves crossing over rugged territory. No husband can consistently meet every expectation. Dreams of romance fade quickly in the daylight.

If we try to find our identity in, or fix our vision on, these things rather than Christ, our heart remains restless, our thoughts unfocused, our arms vacant.

It can be remarkably humbling when we realize (for what may seem like the zillionth time) that only the Lord can be the one perfect Husband; that in Christ alone will our deepest desire for unending love and blissful romance be fulfilled. Nevertheless, we can courageously choose—over and over again: We can open our heart to the Word of God and receive its life-giving truth. We can sit down and surrender our distracting thoughts to receive the quiet stillness of the Holy Spirit's comforting presence. We can stretch out our arms and embrace our loving Redeemer in the midst of our marriage, accepting God's invitation to partner with Him in the vital ministry of blessing our husband.

He First Loved Us

For the thirsty, the hungry, and the distracted, the message of Christ is the same. Jesus speaks of pardon and forgiveness, of joy and peace, given freely to all who look to Him alone to satisfy their innermost needs. "I am the light of the world," is the heart cry of our Savior. "Whoever follows me will never walk in darkness, but will have the light of life" (John 8:12).

Are you trusting Him with your heart today? Can you believe He is bringing you ever closer to being fully conformed to the image of

His Son? We can live in hopeful expectation of that day knowing that He will complete the work He has begun:

> Praise be to the God and Father of our Lord Jesus Christ! In his great mercy he has given us new birth into a living hope through the resurrection of Jesus Christ from the dead, and into an inheritance that can never perish, spoil or fade—kept in heaven for you, who through faith are shielded by God's power until the coming of the salvation that is ready to be revealed in the last time.... Set your hope fully on the grace to be given you when Jesus Christ is revealed. (1 Peter 1:3-5, 13)

"We love because he first loved us" (1 John 4:19). Living in the reality of this great truth is possible for all of us. Yet how easy it is to become discouraged and frustrated in our quest to give and receive love within marriage! In those sublime moments when the Lord blesses us with His compassion, patience, mercy, and grace, we again learn the lesson: Love does not originate in us, but in God. Like it or not, we can love our husband only when God is the source, the substance, and the completion of our love.

Still, we live in a world where it seems perfectly natural to forget whom love really comes from, a world where love and loss intermingle in confusing patterns. Most of us discover early in life this can be quite difficult to sort out, let alone accept or understand.

In the midst of our tears and sorrow, loneliness and rejection, it isn't unusual to feel ourselves standing at a distance from the love our heavenly Father freely offers and calls us to share. Our sadness, hurt, and anger over life's circumstances may cause us to close up our heart rather than more fully reach out to embrace Christ's steady comfort and compassion in the midst of our less-than-perfect, real-life marital circumstances.

We love because He first loved us. Not because we can live free from troubles, trials, and temptations if we love. Not because of what God will do for us if we love Him or what others will (maybe) do for us if we love them. Not even because love is right. Or good. Or best.

"Some may question if God deserves our love or if they might have something to gain by loving him. The answer to both questions is yes, but I find no other worthy reason for loving him except himself," Bernard of Clairvaux, a twelfth-century monk, poignantly observed. "God is clearly deserving of our love especially if we consider who he is that loves us, who we are that he loves, and how much he loves us."[2]

We love because He first loved us—and in loving God, we find our greatest delight, our highest joy, our deepest peace, our brightest vision, our strongest shelter. As we live in His love, we welcome the Lord's unchanging, ever-attentive presence and feel at home dwelling

❧ ❧ ❧ ────────────────────────────────

Dethroning the Sovereigns

Divorce is now a part of everyday American life. It is embedded in our laws and institutions, our manners and mores, our movies and television shows, our novels and children's storybooks, and our closest and most important relationships. Indeed, divorce has become so pervasive that many people naturally assume it has seeped into the social and cultural mainstream over a long period of time. Yet this is not the case. Divorce has become an American way of life only as the result of recent and revolutionary change....

This pervasive decline in the ideal and expectation for long-lasting marriage was perhaps predictable. In every other domain of life, Americans are moving away from lasting relationships and toward limited and contingent commitments.... For years, Prudential Insurance Company asked Americans to seek an affiliation with a durable and dependable company, to buy a "piece of the Rock." Now, in a new advertising campaign, Prudential tells its customers: "Be your own Rock."

If men and women are to find a way to [dismantle the divorce culture], that way can come about only through a change of heart and mind, a new consciousness about the meaning of the commitment itself, and a turning away from the contemporary model of relationships offered by Madison Avenue, Wall Street, or Hollywood.

in His courts of praise, on good days and bad. Revived and refreshed through prayer and worship, we are renewed with the Spirit's power, no matter what marital territory we are today traveling through.

"I trust in your unfailing love," wrote David, who himself encountered staggering highs and lows on the family front (Psalm 13:5). Like God's beloved psalmist, we also gain some understanding of what it means to love ourselves and our husband for Christ's sake—for His uses and purposes, plans and intentions, instead of just our own—as we cling to the Lord's steadfast love through the changing seasons of our life.

It's guaranteed: Life will reliably teach us that married love is more

---

A first step toward that goal will involve recapturing a sense of the purpose of marriage that extends beyond the self. This will require a philosophy and language that offer a richer and more challenging conception of marriage than the one that now dominates our discourse. Our contemporary secular thinking about marriage is a blend of psychotherapy and politics, and its language is one of rights and needs. As the personal ads suggest, the task of finding a partner involves finding someone who will both meet your emotional needs and refrain from infringing on your individual rights. This approach accepts the self as sovereign; a truly "healthy" marriage is one in which neither spouse gives up prerogatives or freedoms. The popular notion of marriage as a fifty-fifty deal is not so much an affirmation of a partnership between equals as a treaty negotiated between two sovereigns who must share space in one castle. And like such arrangements in the political sphere, this kind of arrangement is vulnerable to boundary disputes and border skirmishes, a kind of sniping over whose rights have been violated and who holds advantage. A marital relationship founded on such terms is likely to be both tense and unstable. More centrally, the notion of protecting the essential properties of the self from incursions by another is antithetical to marital commitment in which one must desire and accept as a matter of faith the giving over of oneself to another.[3]—Barbara Dafoe Whitehead

than a feeling, a duty, an act of giving, a moment of forgiveness, a romantic adventure, or a resolute decision to seek our husband's highest good. And it's when our thirst for God grows through unplanned encounters with life's tough terrain and rugged desert places we can best sing: "All my fountains are in you" (Psalm 87:7).

Like many women who have walked this road before us, we discover that if we're willing to keep seeking our Savior, we eventually learn that the Lord's unfailing love for us is far deeper and truer and braver than we ever dreamed it could be—a truth we learn by heart as we follow the Lord with openhearted faith moment by moment, and day by day.

What Do You See?

Vision. A certain way of seeing. The ability to unflinchingly look at the big picture without becoming distracted by myriad minute details. A singleness of eye, a clarity of focus that firmly fixes one's mental, emotional, and spiritual concentration upon one supreme life purpose in spite of heavy opposition from one's enemies. And one's critics.

Have you ever experienced the challenge of keeping your love for the Lord—and your husband—clearly in focus? Do you find yourself being tempted to succumb to the "me first" ethic that predominates in the world around you? If so, you're certainly not alone.

We grow in love under the watchful, tender care of our Good Shepherd when we choose to believe and obey His precepts, commandments, and instructions, increasingly realizing why His burden is light and His yoke easy. And we discover the grace and strength to follow Him in this present age.

Finding our identity in the character and image of Christ, the true source of our identity, transforms our mind and heart. *In Christ we are complete.* Through affirming God's control over the course of our husband's life choices and experiences, we can open our hands and surrender the concerns, irritations, and anxieties to which we cling. In exchange, we receive peace and the wisdom learned in trusting God with every aspect of our life.

In this way, our deep yearning for perfect love—the kind of love only God can give—becomes a source of blessing and holy protection not only for us but also for our husband.

When we feel worried, frustrated, or anxious regarding our husband's attitudes and behavior, it's easy to abruptly adopt a reaction regime. We may deal with our concerns by attempting to manage our husbands' life—in a multitude of different ways—instead of taking our hands off the situation while single-mindedly seeking God's wisdom and relying on His unwavering grace and goodness. (Sound familiar?)

The next time you're faced with this particular temptation, take time out to ask God directly for the Spirit's strength, protection, and sustenance. Turn your deep yearning for perfect love—the kind of love only God can give—into a source of blessing and holy protection not only for you but also for your husband: Affirm God's control over the course of your husband's life choices and experiences; open your hands and surrender the concerns, irritations, and anxieties to which you cling; and receive peace and the wisdom learned in trusting God with every aspect of your life together.

Through blessing and praying for our husband, we surrender our attempts at controlling his life. Releasing our husband more fully to the Lord's loving care—and trusting Him with the consequences—brings greater joy and tranquility to the home front, where it's so desperately needed today.

Remaining in the Lord—abiding in Christ—may seem like a bona fide luxury, given the daily demands placed upon our time, energy, and resources. But we can *choose* to say yes to God.

Though we cannot fully understand the mystery of Jesus' help and the Holy Spirit's sustenance as we walk through life on this side of heaven, we can choose: to patiently abide in Christ for the remainder of our life; to sit at Jesus' feet, quietly listening for His Word in the midst of a discordant chorus of competing voices; to wait on the Lord to renew our strength—before our own strength runs out; to call upon God for direction—especially when the way ahead is unclear; to pray "Thy will be done" as we lift our tear-stained hands in gratitude to the only One who sees our hearts, bears our grief, feels our suffering, knows our needs, and understands our failures.

As we steadily draw closer to Christ, we are inwardly reassured that His plans and purposes are for our good. We see He accepts us in a way that is wonderfully foreign to our earthbound, human experience. Opening our heart to receive the fullness of His love, we trust what the Lord tells us no matter how shadowy our surroundings may appear. His love is constant, unfailing, and never ending. His grace and peace are near.

I can think of no higher goal in life than living to love God, can you? Through Him, may we daily grow in wisdom and grace as we learn how to better love, and bless, our husband.

FOCUS POINTS

- Jesus is actively at work at the center of our marriages—the third strand of the well-weathered cord that cannot be easily broken. His plans and purposes for us are for our good.
- In spite of the rocky journey all marriages must undergo, we can courageously choose, over and over again, to open our hearts to the Word of God and receive its life-giving truth.
- In those sublime moments when the Lord blesses us with His compassion, patience, mercy, and grace, we again learn the lesson: Love does not originate in us, but in God. Like it or not, we can love our husband only when God is the source, the substance, and the completion of our love.
- We love because He first loved us—and in loving God, we find our greatest delight, our highest joy, our deepest peace, our brightest vision, our strongest shelter.

WORDS TO REMEMBER

- Surely goodness and love will follow me all the days of my life, and I will dwell in the house of the LORD forever. (Psalm 23:6)
- The LORD will command His lovingkindness in the daytime; and His song will be with me in the night, a prayer to the God of my life. (Psalm 42:8, NASB)
- For I am confident of this very thing, that He who began a good work in you will perfect it until the day of Christ Jesus.... For it is God who is at work in you, both to will and to work for His good pleasure. (Philippians 1:6; 2:13, NASB)

REAL GUYS

"You know what really turns my crank? When my wife brags on my accomplishments to others. It's not a pride thing; it has to do with the affirmation of my manhood. She was bragging just the other day about the floor my son and I laid, with our melancholy precision. Her amazement that I have been able to rebuild the engine on the Porsche and that it still runs is a good one! Recently I fixed her broken mixer. She hasn't used the broken function on that device for about eight years, and it only took about thirty minutes to figure it out. *Voila!* I guess since we can't go out and slay dragons anymore, fixin' stuff will have to suffice. But it still makes me feel like the hero when I hear her say, 'I can't believe what he's been able to do!' "—Ken

PERSONAL REFLECTIONS

- Reflect on the time you've been married and what the relationship has meant to you over the years. Record your favorite highlights and greatest concerns. Note any areas that need extra attention, identifying things you would like to do differently.
- Express your hopes and desires regarding your husband and your marriage on your next wedding anniversary, recording your reflections on a sheet of paper *for your eyes only*. Store the sheet in a hidden place for one year, and then read the list again. Repeat each year, adding new thoughts and comments to the list on every anniversary.

PRAYERS

Praying God's Blessing for Our Marriage

God, who gives endurance and encouragement, give my husband and me a spirit of unity among ourselves as we follow Christ Jesus, so that with one heart and mouth we may glorify you, the God and Father of our Lord Jesus Christ.—Romans 15:5-6

Praying God's Blessing for My Husband

And, finally, Lord, may I never cease to give thanks for my dear husband when I mention him in my prayers. I keep asking that you, God of our Lord Jesus Christ, the glorious Father, may give my husband the Spirit of wisdom and revelation, so that he may know you better. I pray also that the eyes of my husband's heart may be enlightened in order that he may know the hope to which you have called him, the riches of your glorious inheritance in the saints, and your incomparably great power for us who believe.—Ephesians 1:16-19

Closing Prayer

Here I am, Lord. I'm Yours. My heart is in Your hands—may it always belong to You!

May Your holy peace continually fill and surround our marriage. Protect us from the Evil One, that the enemy may never gain a foothold in our home.

Lord, I ask that you help me bless my husband throughout all the days of our life together. I thank You for joining us together as one in You. By the power of Your Holy Spirit and the light of Your Word, grant me insight, joy, and wisdom, that I may love my husband according to Your design for us.

Lead me, tender Shepherd, with Your strong, steady hand as I follow You moment by moment, that I may live each day in a way pleasing in Your sight.

I love You, Jesus. Thank You for Your unfailing love. Grant me the grace to abide and flourish in Your will, for Your glory. In Jesus' name I pray. Amen.

BLESSINGS NOW

- Turn your deep yearning for perfect love—the kind of love only God can give—into a source of blessing and holy protection not only for you but also for your husband: Affirm God's control over the course of your husband's life choices and experiences; open your hands and surrender the concerns, irritations, and anxieties to which you cling; and receive peace and the wisdom learned in trusting God with every aspect of your life together.
- Keep your sense of humor strong. Laugh and love abundantly.
- Pick your "battles" with your husband prudently. Be willing to take no for an answer.
- Grow in love with your husband under the watchful, tender care of your Good Shepherd, choosing to believe and obey His

precepts, commandments, and instructions, increasingly realizing why His burden is light and His yoke easy.

- Trust God's perfect, unseen, supernatural process as He slowly but surely transforms your mind and heart: *In Christ you are complete.*
- Kiss or hug your husband for at least twenty to thirty seconds. Often. This can be done easily and enjoyably at many different times, in many different places.
- Make a three-stranded cord as a symbol of your marriage: Using three separate pieces of twine, ribbon, raffia, or other decorative cording, braid together one gold strand along with two additional different-colored strands representative of you and your husband. Place this specially woven reminder of God's presence in your relationship in your Bible as a bookmark.
- Bless your husband day by day with these marriage fortifying "one anothers":
  ◊ Have peace with one another (Mark 9:50, NKJV).
  ◊ Love one another (John 13:34).
  ◊ Be devoted to one another (Romans 12:10).
  ◊ Be like-minded one toward another (Romans 15:5, NKJV).
  ◊ Instruct one another (Romans 15:14).
  ◊ Greet one another (Romans 16:16).
  ◊ Serve one another (Galatians 5:13).
  ◊ Be patient, bearing with one another (Ephesians 4:2).
  ◊ Be kind and compassionate to one another, forgiving each other (Ephesians 4:32).
  ◊ Submit to one another (Ephesians 5:21).
  ◊ Lie not to one another (Colossians 3:9, KJV).
  ◊ Admonish one another (Colossians 3:16).
  ◊ Abound in love one toward another (1 Thessalonians 3:12, NKJV).

FOR FURTHER READING

Louise A. Ferrebee, ed. *The Healthy Marriage*. Nashville: Broadman & Holman, 2001.

Joyce Huggett. *Two into One: Relating in Christian Marriage*. Downers Grove, Ill.: InterVarsity, 1981.

Dick Keyes. *Beyond Identity: Finding Your Way in the Image and Character of God.* Ann Arbor, Mich.: Servant, 1984.

Diane Medved. *The Case Against Divorce.* New York: Ivy, 1989.

Dennis Rainey. *One Home at a Time.* Colorado Springs: Focus on the Family, 1997.

Edith Schaeffer. *Common Sense Christian Living.* Nashville: Thomas Nelson, 1983.

Gary Smalley with Al Janssen. *Joy That Lasts.* Grand Rapids: Zondervan, 2000.

R. C. Sproul. *The Intimate Marriage: A Practical Guide to Building a Great Marriage.* Wheaton, Ill.: Loving Books, 1975, 1986.

Scott Stanley. *The Heart of Commitment: Compelling Research that Reveals the Secrets of Lifelong, Intimate Marriage.* Nashville: Thomas Nelson, 1998.

Glenn T. Stanton. *Why Marriage Matters: Reasons to Believe in Marriage in Postmodern Society.* Colorado Springs: Piñon, 1997.

Nick Stinnett; Joe and Alice Beam. *Fantastic Families: 6 Proven Steps to Building a Stronger Family.* West Monroe, La.: Howard Publishing, 1999.

Linda J. Waite and Maggie Gallagher. *The Case for Marriage: Why Married People Are Happier, Healthier, and Better Off Financially.* New York: Doubleday, 2000.

Barbara Dafoe Whitehead. *The Divorce Culture: Rethinking Our Commitments to Marriage and Family.* New York: Vintage, 1996.

Evelyn Eaton Whitehead and James D. *Marrying Well: Stages on the Journey of Christian Marriage.* New York: Doubleday, 1983.

H. Norman Wright. *The Secrets of a Lasting Marriage.* Ventura, Calif.: Regal, 1995.

APPENDIX 6.1
TO YOUR HEALTH

These five key elements of a healthful life will improve your level of well-being and also reduce the effects of stress in your life:

1. A balanced diet: By avoiding excessive sugar, alcohol, and caffeine, processed meats, and monosodium glutamate, you will enhance your ability to cope with daily pressures. Several of these substances have been shown to produce rapid changes in heart rate and contribute to other problems, such as tooth decay, obesity, alcoholism, headaches, and nervousness. In addition, drinking at least two quarts of water and/or water-based, noncaloric fluid (diet soda, coffee, tea, or herbal tea) daily, including in your diet foods rich in complex carbohydrates (whole grain products, fruits, and vegetables), lowering your fat intake, and eating calcium- and protein-rich foods can promote your health and increase your ability to withstand stress.

"Have you ever said, 'I wish I knew what I could do about my allergies, or weight problem, or headaches or blemishes, etc.'?" asks Dr. Susan Negus. "Well, the good news is that there are many steps you can take toward healthy living. It will take some discipline, but your willingness to give up some of the habits and foods that are bad for you and substitute them for good habits and foods will result in a healthier body and, more importantly, prepare you for God's service."[1]

Living a healthful lifestyle involves more than just being "whole" spiritually. It means doing your part in changing your habits and developing an ongoing awareness of how your lifestyle affects your body. You can form realistic expectations and reject our culture's one-dimensional view of the perfect woman. Take your eyes off of your failures, deficiencies, and shortcomings. Give yourself a break! Your amazing body, rich with imperfection as it may be, deserves your tender loving care. Each new day brings multiple opportunities to say yes *and* no to habits and foods that can improve your health.

2. Exercise for energy and enjoyment: Competitive activities or a mind-set that makes you push yourself too hard can increase stress

hormone levels in your body. Consequently, the activities you participate in for enjoyment as well as for fitness are the best forms of exercise. Swimming, walking, dancing, cycling, running, rope-skipping,
and cross-country skiing are all excellent cardiovascular fitness activities for many women. These forms of exercise can significantly reduce
your stress level and improve your sense of well-being, especially when
you engage in them regularly for a minimum of thirty minutes at least
three times a week. They might also just inspire your husband to better health as well: "My wife's discipline in her exercising encourages
me to continue my exercising," says Don, "thus making me feel good
about myself as I keep somewhat in shape."

Not surprisingly, research has definitively shown that strength
training also plays an important role in alleviating the effects of aging
and improving one's quality of life. By regularly engaging in resistance
exercise (specifically prescribed weight lifting and other recommended
strength training methods), you can build bone mass, improve your
balance and flexibility, and enhance weight control.

Truth is, with appropriate, disciplined exercise, you and your husband can build your strength and enhance your energy level. As
energy and stamina increase, everyday life becomes easier. Additionally, the calming effect produced by exercise can ease muscle tension,
reduce anxiety, and relieve pain.

3. A regular bedtime followed by uninterrupted sleep: Irregular sleep
patterns and frequent changes in bedtime schedules can harm your body
by interfering with your ability to dream and reach specific brain wave
patterns during rest. Dreaming allows you to release tension and anxiety;
your metabolism slows down and your muscles relax when you achieve
a deep-sleep state. Since your body and mind are renewed in many different ways when you sleep, getting the rest you need enables you to be
refreshed each night. Adequate sleep and physical rest also enhance the
immune system, as well as reduce the severity of the symptoms associated
with the menstrual cycle and menopause.

4. Appropriate expressions of emotion: It has been said that when
one tries to bury her feelings, she only succeeds in burying them alive.
In other words, ignoring or denying negative feelings does not make

them disappear. When we take our real emotions directly to the Lord, it becomes possible to learn to trust Him more deeply.

"View life as a learning opportunity," Jean Fleming advises. "Ask God what He wants you to learn from the situations you face. Daily Bible reading and prayer prepare us to receive instruction and direction from God. When we set aside specific time to listen, He often encourages us with His presence and promises, and interprets to some degree the circumstances of life. Take advantage of the natural lull after hard times when you're pulling together the pieces to sort through the events and ferret out the lessons.

"The situation we face today can build a greater God-confidence in our life and give us the assurance that in Christ we can tackle what lies ahead. Incident after incident, lesson after lesson, year after year, as we experience God's great faithfulness, grace, and power, we will gain the confidence to say, 'I can do all things through Christ who gives me strength [Philippians 4:13].'"[2]

The Psalms vividly portray this wonderful principle: As David opens his heart to God, we see his heart changing in dramatic ways as he is humbled, strengthened, and renewed in the Lord's presence. This theme is often repeated throughout the Bible. Like David, you too can invite the Lord to know your anxious thoughts and lead you in the everlasting way of His truth (Psalm 139). Learning to be open before God and actively listening to His voice through His Word will bless your life and your marriage.

5. *Quiet times for relaxation:* You can also promote your ability to handle stress on the physical, emotional, and spiritual levels when you take time out to reflect on God's majesty. Taking fifteen or more minutes out of your busy day to set your mind on Christ as you relax in a comfortable position can effectively de-stress your mind, refresh your body, *and* nourish your spirit.

When you sit with your feet up in a recliner, soak in a warm bath, or lie comfortably on a soft, supportive surface, you help your body relax by releasing the muscular tension that has accumulated during the day. With closed eyes, reflect on how much the Lord loves you. Spending time in peaceful prayer with Jesus in this way is yet another means of learning about Him. Rather than only asking for His help and intervention, you will benefit from taking the time to enjoy the Holy Spirit's ever-present comfort and counsel.

Relaxing in this way also stimulates the parasympathetic nervous system (PNS), or quieting response, as a means of countering the effects of stress hormones. Bodily processes slow down and permit the release of powerful chemicals called endorphins. The quieting response is the body's opposite response to the fight or flight reflex. Think about the tingling sensations you feel during a back rub or when someone else brushes your hair. These sensations are related to PNS activity as endorphins and other naturally secreted stress relievers diminish pain and promote a feeling of tranquility. These substances are also released after times of physical exertion.

APPENDIX 6.2
CALM, COOL, AND COLLECTED

In addition to relaxation, there are several other ways you can stimulate your quieting response. Though one of the best ways of provoking the quieting response is through touch, here are twelve things you can do on your own to calm down your nervous system:

1. Warm, leisurely shower or bath
2. Slow breathing: 6-12 breaths per minute
3. Soothing environment: candlelight, dimmed lighting, comfortable room temperature, pillows, loose clothing
4. Relaxing sounds: music, nature sounds, silence
5. Comfortable position that aids in releasing muscular tension
6. Avoidance of worry
7. Reflection on the beauty and majesty of God and His creation
8. Listening to an audio tape of someone reading Psalms
9. Resting in bed while awake
10. Massage: back, neck, face, scalp, arms, legs
11. Contemplative prayer
12. Sitting quietly for fifteen minutes, without distractions or interruptions

As you relax, remember the Lord is with you. Give thanks and praise the Lord for His blessings, entrusting Him with every burden weighing you down. Avoid thoughts that distract you from delighting yourself in God and resting in His presence. Find Bible passages that give you confidence and reassurance—God's promises of peace—and think about them. Give thanks to and praise the Lord for His blessings, entrusting Him with every burden weighing you down.

APPENDIX 8.1
101 GREAT DATES

1. Go for a ride and a talk in the country.
2. Take a bicycle ride. For improving your teamwork, rent a tandem bike.
3. Sit outside in the moonlight, sharing goals and dreams, concluding with thanksgiving for the blessings given to you by God.
4. Work together outdoors, planting trees or gardening.
5. Offer to give your spouse a body massage with scented oil.
6. Get up early together and have coffee or tea out on the patio.
7. Go for a walk in the woods.
8. Go horseback riding and picnic on the trail.
9. Build sand castles at the beach.
10. Go out for dessert.
11. Rent a good movie and eat popcorn together.
12. Bathe together by candlelight.
13. Share a meal at a nice restaurant and go to a play afterwards.
14. Visit a planetarium.
15. Take a dinner train ride.
16. Go sledding or ice-skating. (Take hot cocoa along.)
17. Go for a walk and a talk in a small town with lots of history.
18. Try a water slide or go to a pool for a swim.
19. Get up and watch the sunrise together. (Someone suggested that playing golf at this time of day could be fun, too.)
20. Take a buggy ride together at Christmastime.
21. Take dancing lessons and learn something new about "partnering."
22. Go to the state capitol building for a tour.
23. Attend a high school or college football game (or volleyball, basketball…).
24. Enroll in an adult education class together.

25. Go to a hospital nursery and reflect on the wonder of your child(ren)'s birth(s).
26. Go miniature golfing.
27. Go to a motel for the evening, but return home by midnight.
28. Meet one another for lunch to discuss recent scriptural insights.
29. Rent a sailboat and go out together at a nearby lake.
30. Sit on a blanket at the park, fly a kite, read.
31. Arrange for a hot air balloon ride.
32. Rent a manual paddleboat and go for a short cruise if you live near a lake or a river.
33. Go to an art gallery and browse.
34. Attend a concert, especially one held outdoors so you can curl up and look at the stars while listening to the music.
35. Go bowling.
36. Go on a walk through an area of town with old, interesting homes.
37. Get your hair cut at the same time and place.
38. Get all dressed up and go to an exotic restaurant.
39. Go shopping together—groceries, gifts, or plants.
40. Spend time at a mountain cabin together, reflecting on the majesty of God.
41. Plan and work on a creative project building something.
42. Attend a wedding and reminisce.
43. Take a day trip to an interesting town within an hour's driving distance of your home. Have lunch at the local diner; browse the stores; learn about a little community history.
44. Go to an auction and purchase something funny.
45. Visit antique shops and learn about old furniture.
46. Go for a drive and look at Christmas decorations while sharing memories.
47. Go to a drive-in theater.
48. Plan a surprise date. Blindfold your husband and take him to someplace unusual.
49. Shoot an entire roll of film of one another outdoors.
50. Go on a hayride.

51. Take a walk in the rain under an umbrella.
52. Go to a department store and buy each other some new lingerie and underwear. (No peeking until you get home!)
53. Rent a canoe and go canoeing. Find a quiet spot to read your current favorite book on marriage aloud to one another.
54. Share a plate of nachos at your favorite Mexican restaurant.
55. Set aside an evening for making photo albums or looking at slides.
56. Meet each other for coffee on a workday morning once a month or more, if schedules allow.
57. Go to the library and find a new subject to explore together.
58. Get season tickets for the symphony (or travel series or theater…).
59. Play tennis at a local park.
60. Go Christmas caroling with other couples.
61. Drive out to the country and spot satellites.
62. Go for a hike along trails in a nearby park. Take a Bible and a blanket along, curl up together, and read Song of Songs.
63. Browse in a Christian bookstore and listen to demo tapes.
64. Go to a park and swing on the swings while holding hands.
65. Share a sundae or a soda at a local ice-cream parlor.
66. Stroll along the main street in your town and go window-shopping after all the stores have closed (assuming the streets are safe at night).
67. Take a ride to see the colors change in the autumn or spring.
68. Have friends or family baby-sit your child(ren) at their house. Then go back home and spend the evening in bed.
69. Attend an art, antique, recreation, or craft show.
70. Listen to a favorite mystery on tape while sipping your favorite beverage and sharing a plate of cheese and crackers.
71. Tuck the kids in bed; wait until they're asleep, then have a water gun fight. In your bathing suits.
72. Plan a romantic rendezvous six weeks in advance and keep it a secret between just the two of you.
73. Play board games for the evening: Scrabble, Careers, and Chinese checkers—whatever! Order a pizza.

74. Spend an hour serenading one another with silly and/or serious love songs.
75. Go fishing by moonlight. Forget about the fish. Gaze at the moon and stars instead.
76. Make a scrapbook or put together a photo album about your marriage based on a humorous theme.
77. Go roller-skating.
78. Take a trip to town; buy some penny candy or caramel corn. Share it while relaxing at a park.
79. Set up a pup tent in the backyard and zip two sleeping bags together for an after-dark encounter.
80. Slow dance to your favorite music in the living room with your best nightgown on.
81. Order Chinese egg rolls takeout to eat while snuggled up in bed listening to your favorite music.
82. Construct a family tree containing as many relatives as you can remember, listing any interesting, distinctive, or peculiar characteristics for each.
83. Take turns reading George MacDonald and C. S. Lewis fairy tales aloud together, such as *The Princess and the Goblin*, *The Golden Key*, *The Light Princess*, and *The Chronicles of Narnia*.
84. Study a foreign language together; plan to take a trip to a locale where the language is spoken.
85. Enroll in a noncompetitive fitness program together.
86. Go to an arboretum or an aviary for a stroll.
87. Browse through a bookstore; then go out for some tea or coffee.
88. Buy a Phillip's *Planisphere*, which shows "the principal stars visible for every hour of the year." Carry an old afghan to a hilly spot away from city lights and locate the major constellations.
89. Go wading along a beach.
90. Visit the city fountain and just sit and talk for a while.
91. Cuddle up and watch a thunderstorm from a covered porch or through a large picture window.
92. Do some photography together at a local nature center or zoo.
93. Buy some Archie comic books and read them aloud together.
94. Go out for a late breakfast on Saturday morning.

95. Write a family history book as a late-evening project, instead of watching TV.
96. Audit an art or music appreciation class together at a nearby college or university.
97. Park along a safe deserted road and see what happens.
98. Go to a nice restaurant, but just order an appetizer or dessert.
99. Read poetry together by candlelight—perhaps Elizabeth Barrett Browning and Robert Browning—and conclude with a special prayer for the strengthening of your love for one another.
100. Take an international cuisine cooking class together.
101. Go for a walk in freshly fallen snow. Then take a hot shower together after returning home.

APPENDIX 8.2
HOW TO GIVE A GREAT BACK RUB

Human relationships thrive on touch when it is done appropriately and with respect. We have many examples in the Gospels of Jesus touching those around Him and of His disciples touching Him. I especially like the references to "the disciple whom Jesus loved" leaning back against Jesus at the Last Supper and to His taking the little children in His arms. The "laying on of hands" has great significance throughout the New Testament and continues to be used today in many different denominations during Communion, baptism, ordination, prayers for healing, and requests for special anointing. Through touch we let others know *we care*.

Nurturing, nonsexual physical expressions of love can be a key way of blessing our husbands. Between a husband and wife, the gift of nurturing touch is as significant as it is in any human relationship. If married partners touch one another only in sexual ways or in order to attempt to stimulate one another toward sexual arousal, a marriage can suffer.

Many women have told me of their resentment that their husbands only touch them when they want "something in return." It is certainly true that many men have been raised in homes where cuddling, hugging, snuggling, and putting arms around male family members was uncommon. Discovering new ways of expressing love through touch can be a growing experience for anyone reared in a "low-touch" atmosphere. But learn we must. We can't afford to abandon the caring communication *everyone* needs, whether they're aware of it or not.

It's unrealistic to think that your husband will know how to give you a good back rub if he has never received one himself. Thus, a good way to begin to foster more loving communication through touch in your home is by learning how to give your husband a relaxing massage. In this way, your hands will teach him gently about your love for him and will also "tell" him how you would like him to touch you.

Taking the time to learn this skill is well worth the time and effort.

The principles upon which an effective massage is based are fairly simple to learn and easy to remember. In following these steps, you will rapidly develop an excellent technique and have your husband expressing his appreciation to you even with your first attempt. These steps are:

1. *Reduce the friction* caused by your hands with an agent such as cornstarch or oil. The types of oil that work best are vegetable, nut, or cold-pressed seed oils such as peanut, almond, safflower, or corn oil. You may use them alone or in combination with one another. Scented oils may be obtained through some health food stores or specialty soap shops in eight-ounce or larger containers.

2. When you're ready to begin the massage, *put on some relaxing music and ask your husband to remove his clothing.* Give him a gigantic terry towel or flannel blanket to wrap around himself. When he lies down on his stomach for the back rub, be sure to keep him covered from the buttocks downward. By keeping areas covered that are not a part of the area you are concentrating the massage on, you will keep the focus on the back rub and away from his sexuality. Massage can be incorporated into lovemaking at other times. For learning these techniques as a means of stress reduction, however, it's helpful to agree on avoiding sexual stimulation.

3. *Have him lie on a comfortable surface* at a height that will help you to avoid back strain as you work. If he's lying on his stomach, place a small pillow under his abdomen to reduce back strain for him, if needed. You may also place a rolled towel under the front surface of his ankles to enable his legs to relax. When he is lying on his back, he may enjoy having a doubled up pillow under each knee to reduce back strain.

4. When you massage, *use strokes that conform to the contours of your husband's body* while at the same time applying pressure deep enough to promote circulation but not uncomfortable. Use your hands to "talk" to your husband lovingly, smoothly, and rhythmically.

5. *Stroke in particular patterns* at speeds described in the text. Rhythm and repetition are essential. Stroke without interruption over a specific area until you have completely massaged it.

6. *Pray for your husband while you're touching him.* Let your hands express how you feel about him and view them as a means of conveying not only your love for him, but the Lord's love for him as well. Ask him to do the same for you whenever he gives you a massage. Bless one another through soothing forms of touch.

7. *Obtain feedback from him* to find out what parts of the massage he liked the best and if he would like you to continue by concentrating on specific areas.

8. *Finish the massage one area at a time* by placing your hands flat on the surface that you have completed, pressing in slightly, then lifting up and off the surface. For example, when you have completed the back, place one hand between the shoulders and one hand at the base of the spine, press, then lift both hands at the same time. This quiet signal tells him you are done.

Now that you have learned these tips, you're ready to begin the back rub. Note that the circular and patterned movements you'll be using are directed toward the head and heart, while the long, flowing, relaxing strokes move toward the periphery of the body. In this way, circulation is promoted and relaxation is enhanced. In addition to putting on some soothing music, you might take the phone off the hook to better separate yourselves from the stress of the world outside. This can really be a special time between the two of you, as corny as it may seem. Most of us just get too busy and can use such moments to better appreciate the wonder of our relationships.

Massage Techniques for the Back

1. *Circle sweeps:* With your husband lying on his stomach, place both of your hands at the base of his back on his waist. Be sure to have enough oil on your hands so they glide smoothly over the surface of his skin. Begin to stroke up along the spine (but not on it), using circular movements that move up, over the surface of the back, toward the sides, then back around to the midline. Make the strokes six to eight inches in diameter, applying pressure as you move in an upward direction to the shoulders. It will take four or five circles spiraling upwards to cover the surface of the back.

Once your hands have reached the top, place them at the base of the neck, palms down, and apply gentle pressure as they glide down to the base of the back. Repeat this sequence for two to five minutes or until you feel the muscles in the back release their tension. It may help to think of this counting sequence as you rub: 1 (up), 2 (out), 3 (down) repeated slowly for four or five strokes; on the last stroke—1, 2, 3, center, down, 2, 3, 4.

2. *Hands together:* Now focus your strokes on one side of the back at a time. Place your hands next to each other on the right side of the spine at the base of the back. Put your right hand slightly higher than the left so your right thumb is nearly over the left thumb near the left forefinger. In this way, your left hand will follow the strokes your right hand makes, just as if it is imitating what the right hand is doing. Begin stroking, using the circle sweeps pattern, making sure to glide smoothly over the skin while applying a greater degree of pressure than before. Continue to rhythmically stroke the right side, including the shoulder, for two to three minutes. Repeat this sequence for the same length of time along the left side, leading with your left hand.

3. *Walk-ups:* In this pattern, you will be working closer to the spine, one side at a time. Place the three middle fingers of your right hand next to the right of the base of the spine so they are almost flat. Then put the three middle fingers of your left hand under the base of your right fingers, with your left hand underlying your right palm. Your fingers will be working as a unit and will be touching the back with their fleshiest part. Using circles two inches in diameter, spiral up along the bones of the spine, being sure to avoid putting pressure on the spine itself. You will actually be rubbing only the muscles that lie alongside the bone. The large nerve roots that exit from the spinal cord will be stimulated as well. Each circle can be done in one count, and it will take about sixteen to twenty circles to reach the base of the neck.

Continue upwards along the neck using your right hand only, until you reach the skull. Slide back down to the base of the spine with your hands flat and in the same position you used for Step 2 of the massage. Repeat on the left side, leading with either your left or right middle fingers—whichever is most comfortable. Alternate back and forth in this manner for three to five minutes.

4. *Seesaws:* Place your hands parallel to each other over the top portion of the buttocks in a horizontal position. Your right hand should be on top, with your right thumb lying next to the small finger of your left hand. Following the contour of your husband's body, draw your hands out to the sides. Then slide them over across the back to the opposite sides. Your hands meet only when at the center of the back. The count would be: 1 (right hand moves left/left hand moves right), 2 (right hand moves right/left hand moves left), 1, 2, 1, 2, etc., until the hands reach the shoulders. The movements are nice and easy, and the count is fairly slow. Slide your hands down along the center of the back, in a parallel position, to resume your starting point. Repeat for two to three minutes.

5. *Thumbs-up:* Place your wrists about two inches apart, with your thumbs pointing upwards and your fingers directed toward the sides of the back. Your right fingers will be pointed to the right side and your left fingers to the left. With your hands resting gently on the surface of the back, use the pads on your thumbs to press up along the sides of the spine about three inches at a time in wide arcs. The count for this movement is: 1, press, 2, out—a two-count pattern. Lift the thumbs slightly to return to midline after each stroke while keeping the fingers of both hands resting lightly along the sides. It will take ten to twelve strokes from the base of the spine at the top of the buttocks to the base of the skull. (When you reach the neck, you will be using your thumbs only, with your fingers lifted out and away from his neck. Repeat for several minutes.)

6. *Repeat favorite pattern:* Ask your husband which pattern he enjoyed the most and repeat it for a few minutes. Be creative, as you may develop several patterns of your own after you discover what he likes best.

7. *The harp stroke:* When you have completed Steps 1 through 6, you can finish the back rub with downward stroking along the central area of the back. Beginning near the neck, draw the fingers of your right hand down the back in a stroke that begins at the top and lifts off near the buttocks. As the right hand lifts, the left hand repeats the stroke, so that the pattern is continuous. It will take two counts to complete each stroke. Repeat this for one or two minutes. Place your

right hand at the top of the back, your left hand at the base, and apply a slight pressure to signal the end of the back rub.

Massage Techniques for the Shoulders and Neck

The muscles of the shoulders and neck often carry more than their share of tension compared to other areas of the body. This massage can be done almost anywhere. It is not necessary to massage skin-to-skin, although it is preferable.

1. *Feather stroke:* You may begin this stroke at the top of the head or under the ears by placing your hands lightly on the surface of the skin. With your hands next to each other, or on opposite sides, smoothly stroke downwards, then outwards. Cover the top of the shoulders; then repeat this pattern while moving closer to the center of the back each time. It will take three to five strokes to reach the midline. Repeat this sequence for one to three minutes. (You will be stroking downwards to the level of the shoulder blades each time.)

2. *Kneading dough:* Follow Step 1 with a more vigorous massage that will remind you of kneading bread dough. Start with your hands on both sides of the base of the neck with your thumbs pointing toward the spine and your fingers lying across the sides of your husband's neck. Gently squeeze the muscles lying at the base of the neck while rubbing the muscles carefully between your thumbs and fingers. Move along the muscles that lead from the neck to where the arms are joined to the shoulders. Use circular motions of the thumbs to press his muscles toward your fingers. When you reach the edge of the shoulders, use a long stroke to return back to the neck. Ask your husband how vigorously he wants you to rub, and pray that your hands become stronger! Repeat for several minutes until he indicates the tension is gone. If indicated, spend time on smaller areas that seem to be especially tender or tense. Rub in this manner along the sides of the neck, if needed.

3. *Repeat Step 1:* End this massage by placing your hands on your husband's shoulders, applying pressure for a moment, then lifting off.

APPENDIX 9.1
ARE YOU AVOIDING YOUR HUSBAND?

In the marriage classes I teach I hear many women expressing their desire to enjoy greater sexual intimacy with their husbands. Yet day-to-day realities can make this goal elusive. In exploring the most common reasons for avoiding lovemaking, class participants more easily identify the underlying reasons behind their avoidance. If a woman often tells her husband that it's too cold, too hot, too late, or too early, something more important is likely going on.

Below is an exercise that class participants have found to be an effective starting place to begin to evaluate and address these deeper issues. I encourage you to follow up by reading some books on sexuality written from a Christ-centered perspective. (See "For Further Reading" at the end of chapter 9.) You may also want to talk to your women's ministries coordinator or an older married woman at your church for additional ideas.

Check off any of the reasons you may have had for not making love during the past few months:

____ I felt neglected by my husband.

____ I felt resentful that he expected sex but had not related to me in a loving way.

____ I felt unattractive.

____ I have had difficulty feeling sexually fulfilled during lovemaking.

____ I just wanted to be held or have a back rub without my husband expecting sex afterwards.

____ I was sick and had no interest in sex.

____ I feel that my husband just takes me for granted.

____ My sex drive was low so I couldn't get excited about lovemaking.

____ I resent his enjoying sex while ignoring my needs.

____ I don't know how to tell him how to "pleasure" me or touch me.

____ I have difficulty expressing my needs and end up feeling depressed or resentful.

___ I expect my husband to take responsibility for my sexual pleasure instead of taking responsibility for myself.

___ Sex just isn't fun anymore.

___ I expect my husband to take the lead in lovemaking. I am unable to be the "aggressive partner" in our relationship.

___ I often feel bored or disinterested in lovemaking and participate only to please my husband.

Once you have completed this list, look back over your replies and think about the times lovemaking has been satisfying to you. What do you think made the difference? Have you seen any connection between your active participation in sexual sharing and your husband's ability to enjoy it? Record your responses in your journal.

A 1999 report on female sexual dysfunction (FSD) by the American Medical Association stated that 43 percent of women experience FSD. Yet this all-too-prevalent condition—defined as a lack of interest in sex, lack of genital lubrication or sensitivity, inability to orgasm, or pain during intercourse—typically remains unacknowledged, undiagnosed, and untreated due to the sensitive nature of this topic.

Because so many varied pieces make up the picture of your unique physical, emotional, and spiritual make-up, you might also find it helpful to consider these questions as you further explore your feelings about marital intimacy:

- How did you first learn about sex? Was it a positive or negative experience?
- When you began menstruating, what was your reaction?
- What was your first sexual encounter like?
- How do you feel about your body? When you look in the mirror what do you see?
- Have you discussed any specific areas of concern with your health care provider or counselor?
- What steps do you feel comfortable taking right now to foster the sexual and emotional intimacy you share with your husband?

If you think you may be experiencing FSD, I urge you to seek help from a health care provider and/or counselor with whom you are willing to discuss your concerns.

APPENDIX 9.2
CULTIVATING SEXUAL INTIMACY

The Lord has designed a delightful dimension into the marriage bond—the reciprocal principle. Namely, that as you give pleasure, you enhance your ability to receive pleasure. How does your day-to-day life nurture this principle and nourish the sexual dimension of your marriage relationship? A summary of some helpful ways to cultivate sexual intimacy with your husband is listed below. Check off any steps you think would be helpful to you.

_____ Bathe or shower before going to bed in order to relax.

_____ Read the Psalms to gain a fresh perspective on life.

_____ Take a nap before dinner to have more energy later in the evening.

_____ Obtain help with household and child-rearing responsibilities to lessen the daily load you are carrying.

_____ Have more alone time for quietly reading, writing, praying, thinking, dreaming, etc.

_____ Ask your husband to plan interesting dates for you to enjoy together.

_____ Try something new: Be open to enjoying your body and being more expressive with it during lovemaking. Ask your husband what would please him and try it.

_____ Suggest to your husband that you both read a book on the differences between the way men and women communicate.

_____ Assess how you feel about your body *just as it is*. Take steps to enhance your ability to feel attractive *just as you are* without resorting to drastic diets, an exhausting fitness program, complete beauty makeover, plastic surgery, or expensive clothes.

_____ Reduce daily stress by taking two concrete steps to manage it (time by yourself for at least thirty minutes daily, a long bath, listening to music, etc.).

___ Spend time praying about your lack of sexual interest. Ask the Lord to give you insight, wisdom, and direction concerning your current situation and seek professional advice if needed.

___ Verbalize your feelings with your husband about your joys and frustrations concerning your relationship.

___ Buy a basket and fill it with pampering treats for yourself: facial mask, herbal soaps, foot lotion, bath gel, body cream, etc. Soak in the tub as you use your purchases.

___ On Saturday morning, lie naked with your husband as you quietly hold each other before the day's activities start.

___ Sign up for an exercise class appropriate for your fitness level, or start a walking program to boost your energy.

___ Consider temporarily (or permanently) cutting back on outside obligations.

___ Tell yourself the truth about why you are avoiding lovemaking. (See Appendix 9.1.) Commit yourself to working toward resolving your reluctance.

___ Start a new routine that recognizes your need for middle-of-the-day refreshment: quiet time in the afternoon with tea and a good book; resting with your feet up for thirty minutes or longer; a "silence break" at work with the door closed for twenty minutes.

___ Schedule a spiritual retreat away from home for a few days with your sister or a friend—or by yourself.

___ Keep a journal. Express your feelings about lovemaking in writing.

___ Take more time out to do the things you enjoy.

___ Give each other a massage. (See Appendix 8.2 for some tips on how to give a great back rub.)

___ Read several good books on sexuality written by Christian authors.

___ Go away for the weekend alone together. Use room service for meals. Take along your favorite music, an audio player, and scented candles.

NOTES

Introduction

1. Max Lucado, *Grace for the Moment* (Nashville Nelson Thomas: J. Countryman, 2000), 123.
2. Gary Smalley and John Trent, *The Blessing* (New York: Pocket, 1986), 17-18, 21.
3. Smalley and Trent, 27.

Chapter One

1. Gladys Hunt, *Ms. Means Myself* (Grand Rapids: Zondervan, 1972), 28.
2. Stuart and Jill Briscoe, *Living Love* (Wheaton, Ill.: Harold Shaw, 1993), 122-23.
3. Mike Mason, *The Mystery of Marriage* (Portland, Ore.: Multnomah, 1985), 71-72, 142.
4. Christina G. Rossetti, quoted in *Prayers Ancient and Modern,* comp. by Mary Wilder Tileston (New York: Grosset & Dunlap, 1898), 351.

Chapter Two

1. Henri J. Nouwen, *Bread for the Journey* (San Francisco: HarperSanFrancisco, 1997), December 24.
2. Walter Wangerin, Jr., *As for Me & My House* (Nashville: Thomas Nelson, 1987), 22-24.
3. Smalley and Trent, 190.
4. Jerry Bridges, *Transforming Grace* (Colorado Springs, Colo.: NavPress, 1991), 162-63.

Chapter Three

1. Oswald Chambers, *My Utmost for His Highest* (New York: Dodd, Mead & Co., Inc. 1935), 212.

2. Ruth Bell Graham, *It's My Turn* (Old Tappan, N.J.: Fleming H. Revell, 1982), 74.
3. Dietrich Bonhoeffer, *Life Together* (New York: Harper & Brothers, 1954), 35-36.
4. Neil T. Anderson and Charles Mylander, *Christ-Centered Marriage* (Ventura, Calif.: Regal, 1996), 67.
5. Deborah Newman, *Then God Created Woman* (Colorado Springs: Focus on the Family, 1997), 218, 224-25.

Chapter Four

1. J. I. Packer, *Knowing God*, rev. ed. (Downers Grove, Ill.: Inter-Varsity, 1993), 250.
2. Larry Crabb, *The Marriage Builder* (Grand Rapids: Zondervan, 1982, 1992), 59-61.
3. Thomas à Kempis, quoted in *Prayers Ancient and Modern*, 210.

Chapter Five

1. Anne Morrow Lindbergh, *Gift from the Sea* (New York: Pantheon, 1955), 23-24, 51-52, 55-56.
2. Gary Smalley, *For Better or For Best* (New York: HarperPaperbacks, 1991), 187.
3. Edith Schaeffer, *A Way of Seeing* (Old Tappan, N.J.: Fleming H. Revell, 1977), 200.
4. Augustine of Hippo, quoted in *Prayers Ancient and Modern*, 142. Feminine pronouns added.

Chapter Six

1. Ingrid Trobisch, *The Joy of Being a Woman...And What a Man Can Do* (New York: Harper & Row, 1975), 3-4.
2. Trobisch, 34, 38.
3. Hannah Whitall Smith, *The Christian's Secret of a Happy Life* (Old Tappan, N.J.: Fleming H. Revell/Spire, 1970). Page number unknown.
4. Quoted in *Prayers Ancient and Modern*, 148.

Chapter Seven

1. Lewis Smedes, *Forgive and Forget* (San Francisco: Harper & Row, 1984), xii, 146.
2. Edith Schaeffer, *What Is a Family?* (Old Tappan, N.J.: Fleming H. Revell, 1975), 70-71, 80-81. Italics added.
3. Gary Thomas, *Sacred Marriage* (Grand Rapids: Zondervan, 2000), 13.
4. Jeremy Taylor, quoted in *Prayers Ancient and Modern*, 38.

Chapter Eight

1. Sheldon Vanauken, quoted in *601 Quotes About Marriage & Family*. Compiled by William and Nancie Carmichael (Wheaton, Ill.: Tyndale, 1998), 80.
2. Timothy and Julie Clinton, *The Marriage You've Always Wanted* (Nashville: Word, 2000), 150-51.
3. Basil of Caesarea, quoted in *Prayers Ancient and Modern*, 55.

Chapter Nine

1. Katherine W. Pettis and R. Dave Hughes, "Sexual Victimization of Children: A Current Perspective," *Behavioral Disorders*, February 1985, 137; Marianne Neifert, *Dr. Mom: A Guide to Baby and Child Care* (New York: Signet, 1986), 438-439; Dan B. Allender, *The Wounded Heart* (Colorado Springs: NavPress, 1990), back cover.
2. Judith K. and Jack O. Balswick, *Authentic Human Sexuality* (Downers Grove, Ill.: InterVarsity, 1999), 155.
3. Henry Cloud and John Townsend, *Boundaries in Marriage* (Grand Rapids: Zondervan, 1999), 110-11.
4. Briscoe, 53.

Chapter Ten

1. Chambers, 320.
2. Robert Lewis and William Hendricks, *Rocking the Roles: Building a Win-Win Marriage* (Colorado Springs: NavPress, 1991), 171-72.
3. Lewis and Hendricks, 173-74.

4. Benjamin Jenks, quoted in *Prayers Ancient and Modern*, 121.

Chapter Eleven

1. Chambers, 291.
2. James Houston, *The Transforming Power of Prayer* (Colorado Springs: NavPress, 1996). Page number unavailable.
3. Frances de Sales, quoted in *The Wisdom of the Saints*, ed. Jill Haak Adels (Oxford, Great Britain: Oxford University Press, 1987), 39.
4. John Wesley, quoted in *The Joy of the Saints*, ed. Robert L. Llewelyn (Springfield, Ill.: Templegate, 1989), 257.
5. Jeremy Taylor, quoted in *Prayers Ancient and Modern*, 335.

Chapter Twelve

1. H. Norman Wright, *The Pillars of Marriage* (Ventura, Calif.: Regal, 1979), 8.
2. Bernard of Clairvaux, quoted in *Devotional Classics*, Richard J. Foster and Bryan James Smith, eds. (San Francisco: HarperSan-Francisco, 1990), 40.
3. Barbara Dafoe Whitehead, *The Divorce Culture* (New York: Vintage, 1996), 3, 192-93.

Appendix 6.1

1. Susan Negus, quoted in *Women at the Well* (Fort Worth: Life Publishing, 2001), 131.
2. Jean Fleming, quoted in *A Gentle Spirit*, comp. Ashleigh Bryce Clayton (Uhrichsville, Ohio: Barbour, 1999), March 23.

BIBLIOGRAPHY

Adams, J. *Understanding and Managing Stress.* San Francisco: University Association, 1980.

Ahlem, L. *Living with Stress.* Ventura, Calif.: Regal Books, 1978.

Allender, Dan B. *The Wounded Heart.* Colorado Springs: NavPress, 1990.

Allender, Dan B. and Tremper Longman III. *Intimate Allies.* Wheaton, Ill.: Tyndale, 1995.

Anderson, Neil T. *The Bondage Breaker.* Eugene, Ore.: Harvest House, 1990.

Anderson, Neil T. *Helping Others Find Freedom in Christ.* Ventura, Calif.: Regal, 1995.

Anderson, Neil T. and Charles Mylander. *The Christ-Centered Marriage.* Ventura, Calif.: Regal, 1996.

Arp, David and Claudia. *The Second Half of Marriage.* Grand Rapids: Zondervan, 1996.

Arp, David and Claudia. *The Ultimate Marriage Builder.* Nashville: Thomas Nelson, 1994.

Arterburn, Stephen and Fred Stoeker. *Every Man's Battle.* Colorado Springs: WaterBrook, 2000.

Arterburn, Stephen, Fred Stoeker, and Mike Yorkey. *Every Woman's Desire.* Colorado Springs: WaterBrook, 2001.

Arthur, Kay. *Lord, Is It Warfare?* Portland, Ore.: Multnomah, 1991.

Arthur, Kay, Jill Briscoe, and Carole Mayhall. *Can a Busy Woman Develop Her Spiritual Life?* Minneapolis: Bethany House, 1992.

Augsburger, David. *The Freedom of Forgiveness.* Chicago: Moody, 1970.

Augsburger, David. *When Enough is Enough.* Ventura, Calif.: Regal, 1984.

Augustine of Hippo. *Daily Readings with St. Augustine.* Maura Sée, ed. Springfield, Ill.: Templegate, 1986.

Balswick, Jack O. and Judith K. *Authentic Human Sexuality: An Integrated Christian Approach.* Downers Grove, Ill.: InterVarsity, 1999.

Balswick, Jack O. and Judith K. *The Family: A Christian Perspective of the Contemporary Home*, 2nd ed. Grand Rapids: Baker, 1999.

Beam, Joe. *Becoming One: Emotionally, Spiritually, Sexually*. West Monroe, La.: Howard Publishing, 1999.

Beam, Joe. *Seeing the Unseen: Preparing Yourself for Spiritual Warfare*. West Monroe, La.: Howard Publishing, 2000.

Beckett, Sister Wendy. *Meditations on Joy*. London: Dorling Kindersley, 1995.

Benson, Herbert. *The Relaxation Response*. New York: Avon, 1975.

Bernard of Clairvaux. *The Love of God*. James M. Houston, ed. Portland, Ore.: Multnomah, 1983.

Bevere, Lisa. *You Are Not What You Weigh*. Orlando, Fla.: Creation House, 1998.

Bilicki, Bettie Youngs and Masa Goetz. *Getting Back Together*. Holbrook, Mass.: Bob Adams, 1990.

Blackaby, Henry T. *Experiencing God: How to Live the Full Adventure of Knowing and Doing the Will of God*. Nashville: Broadman & Holman, 1998.

Blackaby, Henry T. and Claude V. King. *Experiencing God: Knowing and Doing His Will*. Nashville: Lifeway, 1994.

Bloesch, Donald G. *Is the Bible Sexist? Beyond Feminism and Patriarchalism*. Westchester, Ill.: Crossway, 1982.

Bloesch, Donald. *The Struggle of Prayer*. San Francisco: Harper & Row, 1980.

Bonhoeffer, Dietrich. *Christ the Center*. New York: Harper & Row, 1960.

Bonhoeffer, Dietrich. *The Cost of Discipleship*. New York: Macmillan, 1963.

Bonhoeffer, Dietrich. *Creation and Fall/Temptation: Two Biblical Studies*. New York: Macmillan, 1972.

Bonhoeffer, Dietrich. *Life Together*. New York: Harper & Brothers, 1954.

Bonhoeffer, Dietrich. *The Martyred Christian*. Ed. Joan Winmill Brown. New York: Macmillan, 1983.

Bonhoeffer, Dietrich. *Psalms: The Prayer Book of the Bible*. Minneapolis: Augsburg, 1970.

Bonhoeffer, Dietrich. *Spiritual Care.* Jay C. Rochelle, ed. Philadelphia: Fortress, 1985.

The Book of Common Prayer. New York: The Church Pension Fund, 1945.

Boteach, Shmuley. *Kosher Sex: A Recipe for Passion and Intimacy.* New York: Doubleday, 1999.

Bounds, E. M. *The Necessity of Prayer.* Grand Rapids: Baker, 1976.

Bowen-Woodward, Kathy. *Coping with a Negative Body Image.* New York: Rosen, 1989.

Brand, Paul and Philip Yancey. *Fearfully and Wonderfully Made.* Grand Rapids: Zondervan, 1980.

Brand, Paul and Philip Yancey. *In His Image.* Grand Rapids: Zondervan, 1984.

Bridges, Jerry. *How to Get Results Through Prayer.* Colorado Springs: NavPress, 1975.

Bridges, Jerry. *The Pursuit of Holiness.* Colorado Springs: NavPress, 1978.

Bridges, Jerry. *Transforming Grace.* Colorado Springs: NavPress, 1991.

Bridges, Jerry. *Trusting God.* Colorado Springs: NavPress, 1988.

Briscoe, Jill. *The One Year Book of Quiet Times with God.* Wheaton, Ill.: Tyndale, 1997.

Briscoe, Jill. *Out of the Storm and into God's Arms: Shelter in Turbulent Times.* Colorado Springs: Shaw/WaterBrook, 2000.

Briscoe, Jill. *Prayer That Works.* Wheaton, Ill.: Tyndale, 2000.

Briscoe, Stuart and Jill. *Living Love.* Wheaton, Ill.: Harold Shaw, 1993.

Brother Lawrence. *The Practice of the Presence of God.* Springdale, Penn.: Whitaker, 1982.

Burroughs, Esther. *Splash the Living Water: Turning Daily Interruptions Into Life-Giving Encounters.* Nashville: Thomas Nelson, 1999.

Carlson, Dwight. *Overcoming Hurts and Anger.* Eugene, Ore.: Harvest House, 1981.

Carmichael, Amy. *A Very Present Help.* Judith Couchman, comp. Ann Arbor, Mich.: Servant, 1996.

Carmichael, Amy. *You Are My Hiding Place*. Minneapolis: Bethany House, 1991.

Carmichael, William and Nancie, comp. *601 Quotes About Marriage & Family*. Wheaton, Ill.: Tyndale, 1998.

Chambers, Oswald. *Daily Thoughts for Disciples*. Grand Rapids: Discovery House, 1994.

Chambers, Oswald. *My Utmost for His Highest*. New York: Dodd and Mead, 1935.

Chambers, Oswald. *Prayer: A Holy Occupation*. Grand Rapids: Discovery House, 1992.

Chapell, Bryan. *Each for the Other: Marriage As It's Meant to Be*. Grand Rapids: Baker, 1998.

Chapman, Gary D. *The Five Love Languages*. Chicago: Northfield, 1995.

Chapman, Gary D. *Hope for the Separated: Wounded Marriages Can Be Healed*. Chicago: Moody, 1996.

Christenson, Evelyn. *What Happens When We Pray for Our Families*. Wheaton, Ill.: Victor, 1992.

Clarkson, Margaret. *Grace Grows Best in Winter*. Grand Rapids: Eerdmans, 1984.

Classics Devotional Bible. Grand Rapids: Zondervan, 1996.

Clayton, Ashleigh Bryce, comp. *A Gentle Spirit*. Uhrichsville, Ohio: Barbour, 1999.

Clinton, Timothy. *Before a Bad Goodbye*. Nashville: Word, 1999.

Clinton, Timothy and Julie. *The Marriage You've Always Wanted*. Nashville: Word, 2000.

Cloud, Henry. *Changes That Heal*. Grand Rapids: Zondervan, 1992.

Cloud, Henry and John Townsend. *Boundaries*. Grand Rapids: Zondervan, 1992.

Cloud, Henry and John Townsend. *Boundaries in Marriage*. Grand Rapids: Zondervan, 1999.

Cloud, Henry and John Townsend. *How People Grow: What the Bible Reveals about Personal Growth*. Grand Rapids: Zondervan, 2002.

Colson, Charles. *Loving God*. Grand Rapids: Zondervan, 1983.

Colson, Charles, and Nancy Pearcey. *How Now Shall We Live?* Wheaton, Ill.: Tyndale, 1998.

Couchman, Judith, comp. *Breakfast for the Soul.* Tulsa, Okla.:
Honor, 1998.

Couchman, Judith, comp. *One Holy Passion: Growing Deeper in Your
Walk with God.* Colorado Springs: WaterBrook, 1998.

Crabb, Larry. *Finding God.* Grand Rapids: Zondervan, 1993.

Crabb, Larry. *Inside Out.* Colorado Springs: NavPress, 1988.

Crabb, Larry. *The Marriage Builder.* Grand Rapids: Zondervan,
1982, 1992.

Crabb, Larry. *Men and Women: Enjoying the Difference.* Grand
Rapids: Zondervan, 1993.

Crabb, Larry. *Shattered Dreams: God's Unexpected Pathway to Joy.*
Colorado Springs: WaterBrook, 2001.

Crabb, Lawrence J., Larry Crabb, and Eugene H. Peterson. *The
Safest Place on Earth.* Nashville: Word, 1999.

Crosby, J. F. *Illusion and Disillusion: The Self in Love and Marriage.*
Belmont, Calif.: Wadsworth, 1976.

Crosby, Robert and Pamela. *Creative Conversation Starters for
Couples.* Tulsa, Okla.: Honor, 2000.

Curtis, Brent and John Eldredge. *The Sacred Romance: Drawing Closer
to the Heart of God.* Nashville: Thomas Nelson, 1997.

de Caussade, Jean-Pierre. *The Sacrament of the Present Moment.* Kitty
Muggeridge, trans. San Francisco: Harper & Row, 1982.

de Caussade, Jean-Pierre. *Self-Abandonment to Divine Providence.*
Springfield, Ill.: Templegate, 1959.

Delitzsch, F. *Commentary on the Song of Songs and Ecclesiastes.* Grand
Rapids: Eerdmans, n.d.

Dobson, James. *Dr. Dobson Answers Your Questions.* Minneapolis:
Grason, 1982.

Dobson, James. *Love for a Lifetime.* Sisters, Ore: Mult-
nomah/Questar, 1993.

Dobson, James. *Straight Talk to Men and Their Wives.* Waco, Tex.:
Word, 1980.

Dobson, James. *What Wives Wish Their Husbands Knew About
Women.* Wheaton, Ill.: Living/Tyndale, 1975.

Dobson, James. *When God Doesn't Make Sense.* Wheaton, Ill.: Tyndale, 1993.

Dobson, James and Shirley. *Night Light: A Devotional for Couples.* Sisters, Ore.: Multnomah, 2000.

Dominian, John. *Christian Marriage.* London: Libra, 1967.

Eldredge, John. *The Journey of Desire: Searching for the Life We Only Dreamed Of.* Nashville: Thomas Nelson, 2000.

Eldredge, John. *Wild at Heart: The Secret of a Man's Soul.* Nashville: Thomas Nelson, 2001.

Elliot, Elisabeth. *God's Guidance.* Grand Rapids: Fleming H. Revell/Baker, 1997.

Elliot, Elisabeth. *A Lamp for My Feet.* Ann Arbor, Mich.: Servant, 1985.

Evans, Debra. *Beauty and the Best.* Colorado Springs: Focus on the Family, 1993.

Evans, Debra. *The Christian Woman's Guide to Personal Health Care.* Wheaton, Ill.: Crossway, 1998.

Evans, Debra. *The Christian Woman's Guide to Sexuality.* Wheaton, Ill.: Crossway, 1997.

Evans, Debra. *Heart & Home.* Westchester, Ill.: Crossway, 1988.

Evans, Debra. *Kindred Hearts: Nurturing the Bond Between Mothers and Daughters.* Colorado Springs: Focus on the Family, 1997.

Evans, Debra. *Soul Satisfaction: For Women Who Long for More.* Wheaton, Ill.: Crossway, 2001.

Evans, Debra. *Women of Character.* Grand Rapids: Zondervan, 1996.

Evans, Debra. *Women of Courage.* Grand Rapids: Zondervan, 1999.

Evans, Patricia, *The Verbally Abusive Relationship.* Holbrook, Mass. Adams Media, 1996.

Everly, G. and D. Girdano, *Controlling Stress and Tension.* Englewood Cliffs, N.J.: Prentice-Hall, 1979.

Fairlie, Henry. *The Seven Deadly Sins Today.* New York: Simon and Schuster, 1978.

Faludi, Susan. *Stiffed: The Betrayal of the American Man.* New York: William Morrow, 1999.

Farrel, Bill and Pam. *Love, Honor & Forgive: A Guide for Married Couples.* Downers Grove, Ill.: InterVarsity, 2000.

Farrell, Warren. *Why Men Are the Way They Are.* New York: Berkley, 1986.

Ferguson, David and Theresa; Chris and Holly Thurman. *Intimate Encounters: A Practical Guide to Discovering the Secrets of a Really Great Marriage*. Nashville: Thomas Nelson, 1994.

Ferguson, Sinclair. *Kingdom Life in a Fallen World*. Colorado Springs: NavPress, 1986.

Ferrebee, Louise A., ed. *The Healthy Marriage Handbook*. Nashville: Broadman & Holman, 2001.

Fleming, Jean. *Feeding Your Soul: A Quiet Time Handbook*. Colorado Springs: NavPress, 1999.

Foster, Richard J. *Celebration of Discipline*. San Francisco: Harper-Collins, 1978.

Foster, Richard J. *Freedom of Simplicity*. San Francisco: Harper & Row, 1981.

Foster, Richard. J. *Prayer: Finding the Heart's True Home*. San Francisco: HarperSanFrancisco, 1992.

Foster, Richard J. *Prayers from the Heart*. San Francisco: HarperSanFrancisco, 1994.

Foster, Richard J. *Richard Foster's Treasury of Christian Discipline*. New York: HarperCollins, 1988.

Foster, Richard J. and Bryan James Smith, Eds. *Devotional Classics*. San Francisco: HarperSanFrancisco, 1990.

Gilder, George. *Men and Marriage*. Gretna, La.: Pelican, 1986.

Gilder, George. *Sexual Suicide*. New York: Quadrangle, 1973.

Gordon, S. D. *Quiet Talks on Prayer*. Westwood, N.J.: The Christian Library, 1984.

Gottman, John, with Nan Silver. *The Seven Principles for Making Marriage Work*. New York: Three Rivers, 1999.

Gottman, John, with Nan Silver. *Why Marriages Succeed or Fail...and How You Can Make Yours Last*. New York: Simon & Schuster, 1994.

Graham, Billy. *Hope for the Troubled Heart: Finding God in the Midst of Pain*. Nashville: Word/Thomas Nelson, 1991.

Graham, Ruth Bell. *It's My Turn*. Old Tappan, N.J.: Fleming H. Revell, 1982.

Gray, John. *Men Are from Mars, Women Are from Venus*. New York: HarperCollins, 1992.

Grayson, Curt and Jan Johnson. *Creating Safe Places.* San Francisco: HarperSanFrancisco, 1991.

Groom, Nancy. *From Bondage to Bonding.* Colorado Springs: NavPress, 1991.

Hall, Laurie. *An Affair of the Mind.* Colorado Springs: Focus on the Family, 1996.

Harrison, Nick, ed. *His Victorious Dwelling.* Grand Rapids: Zondervan, 1998.

Heald, Cynthia. *Becoming a Woman of Freedom.* Colorado Springs: NavPress, 1992.

Hendrix, Harville. *Getting the Love You Want.* New York: Harper-Perennial, 1988.

Henry, M. *Matthew Henry's Commentary,* Vol. 1. Grand Rapids: Baker, 1983.

Hersh, Sharon A. *Bravehearts: Unlocking the Courage to Love with Abandon.* Colorado Springs: WaterBrook, 2000.

Houston, James. *The Heart's Desire.* Colorado Springs: NavPress, 1996.

Houston, James. *In Pursuit of Happiness: Finding Genuine Fulfillment in Life.* Colorado Springs: NavPress, 1996.

Houston, James. *The Transforming Power of Prayer.* Colorado Springs: NavPress, 1996.

Howard, J. G. *The Trauma of Transparency.* Portland, Ore.: Multnomah, 1979.

Huggett, Joyce. *The Joy of Listening to God.* Downers Grove, Ill.: InterVarsity, 1986.

Huggett, Joyce. *Learning the Language of Prayer.* New York: Crossroad, 1986.

Huggett, Joyce. *Listening to God.* London: Hodder & Stoughton, 1986.

Huggett, Joyce. *Listening to Others.* Downers Grove, Ill.: InterVarsity, 1988.

Huggett, Joyce. *Two into One: Relating in Christian Marriage.* Downers Grove, Ill.: InterVarsity, 1981.

Hunt, Gladys. *Honey for a Woman's Heart: Growing Your World Through Reading Great Books.* Grand Rapids: Zondervan, 2002.

Hunt, Gladys. *Ms. Means Myself.* Grand Rapids: Zondervan, 1972.
Hunter, W. Bingham. *The God Who Hears.* Downers Grove, Ill.: InterVarsity, 1986.
Hurley, James B. *Man and Woman in Biblical Perspective.* Grand Rapids: Zondervan, 1981.
Hybels, Bill. *Tender Love: God's Gift of Sexual Intimacy.* Chicago: Moody, 1993.
Hybels, Bill and Lynne. *Fit to Be Tied.* Grand Rapids: Zondervan, 1991.
Janssen, Al. *The Marriage Masterpiece.* Wheaton, Ill.: Tyndale. 2001.
Jeffers, Susan. *Opening Our Hearts to Men.* New York: Fawcett Columbine, 1989.
Johnson, Jan. *Enjoying the Presence of God.* Colorado Springs: NavPress, 1996.
Johnson, Jan. *When the Soul Listens: Finding Rest and Direction in Contemplative Prayer.* Colorado Springs: NavPress, 1999.
Joy, Donald M. *Bonding: Relationships in the Image of God.* Waco, Tex.: Word, 1985.
Joy, Donald M. *Re-bonding: Preventing and Restoring Damaged Relationships.* Waco, Tex.: Word, 1986.
Joy and Strength, comp. Mary W. Tileston. New York: Barnes & Noble, 1993.
The Joy of the Saints, ed. Robert Llewelyn. Springfield, Ill.: Templegate, 1989.
Keener, Craig S. *The IVP Bible Background Commentary: New Testament.* Downers Grove, Ill.: InterVarsity, 1993.
Kent, Carol. *Secret Longings of the Heart.* Colorado Springs: NavPress, 1990.
Keyes, Dick. *Beyond Identity: Finding Your Way in the Image and Character of God.* Ann Arbor, Mich.: Servant, 1984.
Kinder, Melvin and Connell Cowan. *Husbands and Wives.* New York: Signet, 1989.
Kirkpatrick, A. F. *The Book of Psalms.* Grand Rapids: Baker, 1982.
Krasnow, Iris. *Surrendering to Marriage: Husbands, Wives, and Other Imperfections.* New York: Hyperion, 2002.
Kreeft, Peter. *Back to Virtue.* San Francisco: Ignatius, 1992.

Kreeft, Peter. *Making Sense out of Suffering*. Ann Arbor, Mich.: Servant, 1986.

Laaser, Mark. *Faithful and True*. Grand Rapids: Zondervan, 1992.

LaHaye, Tim. *Understanding the Male Temperament*. Grand Rapids: Fleming H. Revell/Baker, 1996.

Landis, Mary and Judson. *Building a Successful Marriage*. Englewood Cliffs, N.J.: Prentice Hall, 1958.

Lasch, Christopher. *The Culture of Narcissism*. New York: W. W. Norton, 1979.

Leman, Kevin. *Making Sense of the Men in Your Life*. Nashville: Thomas Nelson, 2001.

L'Engle, Madeleine. *Two-Part Invention*. San Francisco: HarperSanFrancisco, 1988.

Lewis, C. S. *C. S. Lewis on Love*, comp. Lesley Walmsley. Nashville: Thomas Nelson, 1998.

Lewis, C. S. *The Four Loves*. London: Geoffrey Bles, 1960.

Lewis, C. S. *The Great Divorce*. New York: Macmillan, 1946.

Lewis, C. S. *Letters to Malcolm: Chiefly on Prayer*. New York: Harvest/Harcourt Brace Jovanovich, 1964.

Lewis, C. S. *The Lion, the Witch and the Wardrobe*. New York: Macmillan, 1950.

Lewis, C. S. *Mere Christianity*. New York: Macmillan, 1943.

Lewis, C. S. *Miracles*. New York: Macmillan, 1960.

Lewis, C. S. *The Problem of Pain*. New York: Macmillan, 1977.

Lewis, C. S. *Reflections on the Psalms*. New York: Harvest/HBJ, 1958.

Lewis, C. S. *The Screwtape Letters*. New York: Macmillan, 1948.

Lewis, C. S. *Screwtape Proposes a Toast*. London: Fontana, 1965.

Lewis, C. S. *The Seeing Eye*. Walter Hooper, ed. New York: Ballantine, 1967.

Lewis, C. S. *The Visionary Christian*. Chad Walsh, ed. New York: Macmillan, 1981.

Lewis, C. S. *The Weight of Glory*. Grand Rapids: Eerdmans, 1949.

Lewis, Robert and William Hendricks. *Rocking the Roles: Building a Win-Win Marriage*. Colorado Springs: NavPress, 1991.

Linamen, Karen Scalf. *Pillow Talk*. Grand Rapids: Fleming H. Revell/Baker, 1996.

Lindbergh, Anne Morrow. *Gift from the Sea*. New York: Pantheon, 1955.

Linn, Dennis, Sheila Fabricant Linn, and Matthew Linn. *Don't Forgive Too Soon*. New York: Paulist, 1997.

Lloyd-Jones, D. Martyn. *The Cross*. Christopher Catherwood, ed. Wheaton, Ill.: Crossway, 1986.

Lloyd-Jones, D. Martyn. *Joy Unspeakable: Power and Renewal in the Holy Spirit*. Christopher Catherwood, ed. Wheaton, Ill.: Shaw, 1984.

Lotz, Anne Graham. *The Vision of His Glory*. Nashville: Word, 1997.

Lowery, Fred. *Covenant Marriage: Staying Together for Life*. West Monroe, La.: Howard Publishing, 2002.

Lucado, Max. *Grace for the Moment*. Nashville: Thomas Nelson/J. Countryman, 2000.

Luciano, Mark and Christopher Merris. *If Only You Would Change*. Nashville: Thomas Nelson, 1992.

Lush, Jean. *Women and Stress*. Grand Rapids: Fleming H. Revell/Baker, 1992.

Macaulay, Susan Schaeffer. *How to Be Your Own Selfish Pig*. Elgin, Ill.: David C. Cook, 1982.

MacDonald, Gail. *High Call, High Privilege*. Peabody, Mass.: Hendrickson, 1998.

MacDonald, Gail. *A Step Father and Higher*. Sisters, Ore.: Multnomah, 1992.

MacDonald, George. *At the Back of the North Wind*. London: J. M. Dent and Sons, 1956.

Mace, David and Vera. *How to Have a Happy Marriage*. Nashville: Abingdon, 1977.

Macy, Howard. *Rhythms of the Inner Life*. Old Tappan, N.J.: Fleming H. Revell, 1988.

Manning, Brennan. *The Wisdom of Tenderness: What Happens When God's Fierce Mercy Transforms Our Lives*. San Francisco: HarperSanFrancisco, 2002.

Marshall, Catherine. *Beyond Our Selves*. Grand Rapids: Chosen/Baker, 2001.

Mason, Mike. *The Mystery of Marriage*. Portland, Ore.: Multnomah, 1985.

May, Gerald. *Addiction and Grace: Love and Spirituality in the Healing of Addictions.* New York: HarperCollins, 1991.

McCartney, Bill and Lyndi; Connie Neal. *Sold Out Two-Gether: A Couples Workbook.* Nashville: Word, 1999.

McDowell, Josh. *Building Your Self-Image.* Wheaton, Ill.: Tyndale House/Living Books, 1984.

McDowell, Josh and Paul Lewis. *Givers, Takers & Other Kinds of Lovers.* Wheaton, Ill.: Living/Tyndale, 1980.

McGee, Roger. *The Search for Significance.* Houston: Rapha, 1990.

McGrath, Alister, ed. *Christian Spirituality.* Oxford: Blackwell, 1999.

McGrath, Alister. *Understanding Jesus.* Grand Rapids: Zondervan, 1988.

McIntyre, David M. *The Hidden Life of Prayer.* Denville, N.J.: Dimension, 1971.

McKenna, Christine A. *Love, Infidelity, and Sexual Addiction.* St. Meinrad, Ind.: Abbey Press, 1992.

McManus, Michael J. *Marriage Savers.* Grand Rapids: Zondervan, 1993.

McVey, Steve. *Grace Rules.* Eugene, Ore.: Harvest House, 1998.

McVey, Steve. *Grace Walk.* Eugene, Ore.: Harvest House, 1995.

Mead, Frank S., ed. *12,000 Religious Quotations.* Grand Rapids: Baker, 1989.

Means, Marsha. *Living with Your Husband's Secret Wars.* Grand Rapids: Fleming H. Revell/Baker, 1999.

Means, Patrick. *Men's Secret Wars.* Grand Rapids: Fleming H. Revell, 1996.

Medved, Diane. The *Case Against Divorce.* New York: Ivy, 1989.

Miles, Herbert J. *Sexual Happiness in Marriage.* Grand Rapids: Zondervan, 1967.

Miller, J. Keith. *A Hunger for Healing: The Twelve Steps as a Classic Model for Christian Spiritual Growth.* San Francisco: HarperSanFrancisco, 1991.

Miller, J. Keith. *Sin: Overcoming the Ultimate Deadly Addiction.* New York: Harper & Row, 1987.

Moore, Beth. *Praying God's Word: Breaking Free from Spiritual Strongholds.* Nashville: Broadman & Holman, 2000.

Moore, Carey and Pamela Rosewell Moore. *What Happens When Husbands and Wives Pray Together?* Grand Rapids: Fleming H. Revell/Baker, 1992.

More, Hannah. *Practical Piety.* New York: D. Appleton, 1854.

Morley, Patrick. *The Man in the Mirror.* Grand Rapids: Zondervan, 1997.

Morley, Patrick. *Two-Part Harmony.* Nashville: Thomas Nelson, 1994.

Moulton, R. G. *Lyric Idyl: Solomon's Song in the Literary Study of the Bible.* London: Isbiter, 1903.

Mulholland, M. Robert. *Shaped by the Word: The Power of Scripture in Spiritual Formation.* Nashville: Upper Room, 1985.

Munger, Robert Boyd. *My Heart—Christ's Home.* Downers Grove, Ill.: InterVarsity, 1992.

Murray, Andrew. *Abide in Christ.* Old Tappan, N.J.: Spire/Fleming H. Revell, n.d., 1895

Murray, Andrew. *Humility: The Beauty of Holiness.* Fort Washington, Penn.: Christian Literature Crusade, 1997.

Murray, Andrew. *Waiting on God.* Chicago: Moody, n.d.

Murray, Andrew. *With Christ in the School of Prayer.* Old Tappan, N.J.: Fleming H. Revell, 1975.

My Heart Sings, comp. Joan Winmill Brown. Waco, Tex.: Word, 1987.

Narramore, Bruce. *You're Someone Special.* Grand Rapids: Zondervan, 1978.

Navigator Studies. *God's Design for the Family,* books 1-4. Colorado Springs: NavPress, 1980.

Nee, Watchman. *The Latent Power of the Soul.* New York: Christian Fellowship, 1972.

Neifert, Marianne. *Dr. Mom: A Guide to Baby and Child Care.* New York: Signet, 1986.

Nieder, John and Thomas M. Thompson. *Forgive and Love Again: Healing Wounded Relationships.* Eugene, Ore.: Harvest House, 1991.

Nieder, John and Teri. *The Marriage Maker: The Holy Spirit and the Hidden Power of Becoming One.* Eugene, Ore.: Harvest House, 1996.

The New Encyclopedia of Christian Quotations, comp. Mark Water.
Grand Rapids: Baker, 2000.

Newman, Deborah. *Then God Created Woman*. Colorado Springs:
Focus on the Family, 1997.

Nieder, John and Thomas M. Thompson. *Forgive and Love Again: Healing Wounded Relationships*. Eugene, Ore.: Harvest House, 1991.

Nieder, John and Teri. *The Marriage Maker: The Holy Spirit and the Hidden Power of Becoming One*. Eugene, Ore.: Harvest House, 1996.

Nouwen, Henri J. M. *Bread for the Journey*. San Francisco: HarperSanFrancisco, 1997.

Nouwen, Henri J. M. *Making All Things New: An Invitation to the Spiritual Life*. New York: Harper & Row, 1981.

Nouwen, Henri J. M. *The Only Necessary Thing: Living a Prayerful Life*. Wendy Wilson Greer, ed. New York: Crossroad, 1999.

Nouwen, Henri J. M. *Turn My Mourning into Dancing: Moving Through Hard Times with Hope*. Compiled and edited by Timothy Jones. Nashville: Word, 2001.

Nouwen, Henri J. M. *The Way of the Heart*. New York: Ballantine, 1981.

Nouwen, Henri J. M. *With Open Hands*. Notre Dame, Ind.: Ave Maria, 1972.

O'Brien, Gene and Judith. *Couples Praying*. New York: Paulist, 1986.

Omartian, Stormie. *Finding Peace for Your Heart: A Woman's Guide to Emotional Health*. Nashville: Thomas Nelson, 1991.

O'Mathúna, Dónal and Walt Larimore. *Alternative Medicine: The Christian Handbook*. Grand Rapids: Zondervan, 2001.

On Being Christian. Armand Eisen, ed. Kansas City, Mo.: Ariel/Andrews McMeel, 1995.

One Holy Passion, comp. Judith Couchman. Colorado Springs: WaterBrook, 1998.

Ortlund, Anne. *Disciplines of the Beautiful Woman*. Waco, Tex.: Word, 1977.

Packer, J. I. *Knowing God*, rev. ed. Downers Grove, Ill.: InterVarsity, 1993.

Page, Susan. *How One of You Can Bring the Two of You Together.* New York: Broadway, 1997.

Palms, Roger C. *The Pleasure of His Company.* Wheaton, Ill.: Tyndale, 1982.

Parrott, Les. *The Control Freak: Coping with Those Around You, Taming the One Within.* Wheaton, Ill.: Tyndale, 2000.

Parrott, Les and Leslie. *Becoming Soul Mates.* Grand Rapids: Zondervan, 1995.

Parrott, Les and Leslie. *Saving Your Marriage Before It Starts: Seven Questions to Ask Before (and After) You Marry.* Grand Rapids: Zondervan, 1995.

Parshall, Janet and Craig. *Tough Faith: Trusting God in Troubled Times.* Eugene, Ore.: Harvest House, 1999.

Passno, Diane. *Feminism: Mystique or Mistake?* Wheaton, Ill.: Tyndale, 2000.

Paul, Benjamin. *Health, Culture, and Community.* New York: Russell Sage, 1955.

Peace, Richard. *Contemplative Bible Reading: Experiencing God Through Scripture.* Colorado Springs: NavPress, 1996.

Peck, M. Scott. *The Road Less Traveled.* New York: Simon & Schuster, 1978.

Penner, Clifford and Joyce. *52 Ways to Have Fun, Fantastic Sex.* Nashville: Thomas Nelson, 1994.

Penner, Clifford and Joyce. *Getting Your Sex Life off to a Great Start.* Nashville: Thomas Nelson, 1994.

Penner, Clifford and Joyce. *A Gift for All Ages.* Waco, Tex.: Word, 1986.

Penner, Clifford and Joyce. *The Gift of Sex.* Waco, Tex.: Word, 1981.

Penner, Clifford and Joyce. *Restoring the Pleasure.* Waco, Tex.: Word, 1993.

Perkins, Bill. *When Good Men Are Tempted.* Grand Rapids: Zondervan, 1997.

Petersen, J. Allan. *The Myth of the Greener Grass.* Wheaton, Ill.: Tyndale, 1983.

Petersen, William J. *C. S. Lewis Had a Wife.* Wheaton, Ill.: Living/Tyndale, 1986.

Petersen, William J. *Harriet Beecher Stowe Had a Husband.* Wheaton, Ill.: Tyndale, 1983.

Petersen, William J. *Martin Luther Had a Wife.* Wheaton, Ill.: Tyndale, 1983.

Peterson, Eugene H. *Answering God: The Psalms As Tools for Prayer.* San Francisco: HarperSanFrancisco, 1989.

Peterson, Eugene H. *Earth and Altar: The Community of Prayer in a Self-Bound Society.* Downer's Grove, Ill.: InterVarsity, 1985.

Peterson, Eugene H. *A Long Obedience in the Same Direction: Discipleship in an Instant Society.* Downers Grove, Ill.: InterVarsity, 1985.

Peterson, Eugene H. *Praying with Jesus: A Year of Daily Prayer and Reflections on the Words and Actions of Jesus.* San Francisco: HarperSanFrancisco, 1993.

Pettis, Katherine W. and R. Dave Hughes, "Sexual Victimization of Children: A Current Perspective," *Behavioral Disorders,* February 1985.

Piper, John. *Desiring God: Meditations of a Christian Hedonist.* Portland, Ore.: Multnomah, 1986.

Pittman, Frank. *Private Lies: Infidelity and the Betrayal of Intimacy.* New York: W. W. Norton, 1989.

Powers, Marie. *Shame: Thief of Intimacy.* Lynwood, Wash.: Aglow, 1996.

Prayers Ancient and Modern, comp. Mary Wilder Tileston. New York: Grosset & Dunlap, 1897.

Rainey, Dennis. *One Home at a Time.* Colorado Springs: Focus on the Family, 1997.

Rainey, Dennis. *Starting Your Marriage Right.* Nashville: Thomas Nelson, 2000.

Rainey, Dennis. *We Still Do.* Nashville: Thomas Nelson, 2001.

Rainey, Dennis and Barbara. *Moments Together for Couples.* Ventura, Calif.: Regal, 1995.

Rainey, Dennis and Barbara. *The New Building Your Mate's Self-Esteem.* Nashville: Thomas Nelson, 1995.

Richards, Lawrence O. *The Bible Reader's Companion.* Wheaton, Ill.: Victor, 1991.

Robinson, Constance. *Passion and Marriage*. London: S.P.C.K., 1965.

Rosberg, Gary. *The Do-It-Yourself Relationship Mender: A Remarkable Remedy for Unresolved Conflict*. Colorado Springs: Focus on the Family, 1992, 1995.

Rosberg, Gary and Barbara. *The Five Love Needs of Men and Women*. Wheaton, Ill.: Tyndale, 2000.

Rosenau, Douglas. *A Celebration of Sex: A Guide to Enjoying God's Gift of Sexual Intimacy*. Nashville: Thomas Nelson, 1996.

Russell, Diane. *The Secret Trauma: Incest in the Lives of Girls and Women*. New York: Basic, 1986.

Ryken, Leland. *Culture in Christian Perspective*. Portland, Ore.: Multnomah, 1986.

Sanders, J. Oswald. *Enjoying Intimacy with God*. Chicago: Moody, 1980.

Scarf, Maggie. *Intimate Partners*. New York: Ballantine, 1987.

Schaef, Ann Wilson. *When Society Becomes an Addict*. San Francisco: Harper & Row, 1987.

Schaeffer, Edith. *Affliction*. Old Tappan, N.J.: Fleming H. Revell, 1978.

Schaeffer, Edith. *The Art of Life*. Wheaton, Ill.: Crossway, 1987.

Schaeffer, Edith. *Common Sense Christian Living*. Nashville: Thomas Nelson, 1983.

Schaeffer, Edith. *Lifelines: The Ten Commandments for Today*. Westchester, Ill.: Crossway 1983.

Schaeffer, Edith. *A Way of Seeing*. Old Tappan, N.J.: Fleming H. Revell, 1977.

Schaeffer, Edith. *What is a Family?* Old Tappan, N.J.: Fleming H. Revell, 1975.

Schaeffer, Francis. *The Francis Schaeffer Trilogy*. Wheaton, Ill.: Crossway, 1990.

Schaeffer, Francis. *Genesis in Space and Time*. Downers Grove, Ill.: InterVarsity, 1972.

Schaeffer, Francis. *How Should We Then Live?* Old Tappan, N.J.: Fleming H. Revell, 1976.

Schaeffer, Francis. *True Spirituality*. Wheaton, Ill.: Tyndale, 1971.

Schaumberg, Harry W. *False Intimacy: Understanding the Struggle of Sexual Addiction.* Colorado Springs: NavPress, 1994.

Schlink, M. Basilea. *Repentance: The Joy-filled Life.* Grand Rapids: Zondervan, 1968.

Schlossberg, Herbert. *Idols for Destruction.* Wheaton, Ill.: Crossway, 1990.

Schneider, Jennifer. *Back from Betrayal.* New York: Ballantine, 1988.

Schramm, Edward W., ed. *At Jesus' Feet.* Minneapolis: Augsburg, 1936.

Seamands, David. *Healing for Damaged Emotions.* Wheaton, Ill.: Victor, 1981.

Seamands, David. *Healing Grace: Letting God Free You from the Performance Trap.* Wheaton, Ill.: Victor, 1988.

Seid, Roberta Pollack. *Never Too Thin: Why Women Are at War with Their Bodies.* New York: Prentice Hall, 1989.

Selye, Hans. *Stress: General Adaptation Syndrome and the Disease of Adaptation.* Montreal: ACTA, 1950.

Shalit, Wendy. *A Return to Modesty: Discovering the Lost Virtue.* New York: Free Press, 1999.

Shaw, Luci. *Water My Soul.* Grand Rapids: Zondervan, 1998.

Shedd, Charlie W. *Letters to Karen.* New York: Avon, 1965.

Sheets. Dutch. *Intercessory Prayer.* Ventura, Calif.: Regal, 1997.

Sherrer, Quinn and Ruthanne Garlock. *The Spiritual Warrior's Prayer Guide.* Ann Arbor, Mich.: Vine/Servant, 1992.

Sherrer, Quinn and Ruthanne Garlock. *A Woman's Guide to Spiritual Warfare.* Ann Arbor, Mich.: Vine/Servant, 1991.

Small, Dwight Hervey. *Design for Christian Marriage.* Old Tappan, N.J.: Spire/Fleming H. Revell, 1969.

Smalley, Gary. *For Better or for Best.* New York: HarperPaperbacks, 1991.

Smalley, Gary. *Hidden Keys of a Loving, Lasting Marriage.* Grand Rapids: Zondervan, 1988.

Smalley, Gary. *If Only He Knew.* New York: Harper, 1979.

Smalley, Gary. *Making Love Last Forever.* Nashville: Word, 1996.

Smalley, Gary. *Secrets to Lasting Love.* New York: Simon & Schuster, 2000.

Smalley, Gary and Norma. *It Takes Two to Tango: More than 250 Secrets to Communication, Romance and Intimacy in Marriage.* Colorado Springs: Focus on the Family, 1997.

Smalley, Gary and John Trent. *The Blessing.* New York: Pocket, 1986.

Smalley, Gary and John Trent. *The Gift of the Blessing.* Nashville: Thomas Nelson, 1993.

Smalley, Gary and John Trent. *The Hidden Value of a Man.* Colorado Springs: Focus on the Family, 1992.

Smalley, Gary and John Trent. *The Language of Love.* New York: Pocket, 1988.

Smalley, Gary and John Trent. *Love Is a Decision: Proven Techniques to Keep Your Marriage Alive and Healthy.* Nashville: Word, 1989.

Smalley, Gary and John Trent. *The Two Sides of Love.* Colorado Springs: Focus on the Family, 1990.

Smalley, Gary with Al Janssen. *Joy That Lasts.* Grand Rapids: Zondervan, 2000.

Smedes, Lewis. *The Art of Forgiving.* Nashville: Moorings, 1996.

Smedes, Lewis. *Forgive and Forget.* San Francisco: Harper & Row, 1984.

Smedes, Lewis. *Sex for Christians.* Grand Rapids: Eerdmans, 1976.

Smedes, Lewis. *Shame and Grace: Healing the Shame We Don't Deserve.* New York: HarperCollins, 1993.

Smith, Hannah Whitall. *The Christian's Secret of a Happy Life.* Old Tappan, N.J.: Fleming H. Revell/Spire, 1970.

Smith, Hannah Whitall. *The Unselfishness of God.* Princeton, N.J.: Littlebrook, 1987.

Snyder, Chuck. *Men: Some Assembly Required.* Colorado Springs: Focus on the Family, 1995.

Snyder, Chuck and Barb. *Incompatibility: Still Grounds for a Great Marriage.* Sisters, Ore.: Multnomah, 1999.

Snyder, Howard. *The Community of the King.* Downers Grove, Ill.: InterVarsity, 1977.

Springle, Pat. *Codependency: A Christian Perspective.* Houston: Rapha, 1989.

Sproul, R. C. *The Holiness of God.* Wheaton, Ill.: Tyndale, 1985.

Sproul, R. C. *The Intimate Marriage: A Practical Guide to Building a Great Marriage.* Wheaton, Ill.: Loving Books, 1975, 1986.

Sproul, R. C. *Pleasing God.* Wheaton, Ill.: Tyndale, 1988.

Sproul, R. C. *The Soul's Quest for God.* Wheaton, Ill.: Tyndale, 1992.

Spurgeon, Charles Haddon. *All of Grace.* Springdale, Penn.: Whitaker, 1983.

Spurgeon, Charles Haddon. *Morning and Evening.* Grand Rapids: Zondervan, 1960.

Spurgeon, Charles Haddon. *Psalms.* David Otis Fuller, ed. Grand Rapids: Kregel, 1968.

Spurgeon, Charles Haddon. *The Treasury of David.* London: Passmore and Alabaster, 1871.

Stafford, Tim. *Knowing the Face of God: The Search for a Personal Relationship with God.* Grand Rapids: Zondervan, 1986.

Stanley, Scott. *The Heart of Commitment: Compelling Research that Reveals the Secrets of Lifelong, Intimate Marriage.* Nashville: Thomas Nelson, 1998.

Stanley, Scott, Daniel Trathen, Savanna McCain, and Milt Bryan. *A Lasting Promise: A Christian Guide to Fighting for Your Marriage.* San Francisco: Jossey-Bass, 1998.

Stanton, Glenn T. *Why Marriage Matters: Reasons to Believe in Marriage in Postmodern Society.* Colorado Springs: Piñon, 1997.

Steere, Douglas V., ed. *Great Devotional Classics.* Nashville: Upper Room, 1961.

Stinnett, Nick and Nancy; Donnie Hilliard. *Magnificent Marriage: 10 Beacons Show the Way to Marriage Happiness.* West Monroe, La.: Howard Publishing, 2000.

Stinnett, Nick; Joe and Alice Beam. *Fantastic Families: 6 Proven Steps to Building a Stronger Family.* West Monroe, La.: Howard Publishing, 1999.

Stott, John R. W. *Baptism and Fullness: The Work of the Holy Spirit Today.* Downers Grove, Ill.: InterVarsity, 1976.

Stott, John R. W. *Basic Christianity.* Downers Grove, Ill.: InterVarsity, 1971.

Stott, John R. W. *Basic Introduction to the New Testament.* Downers Grove, Ill.: InterVarsity, 1964.

Stott, John R. W. *Christian Counter-Culture: The Message of the Sermon on the Mount.* Downers Grove, Ill.: InterVarsity, 1978.

Stott, John R. W. *Involvement: Social and Sexual Relationships in the Modern World.* Old Tappan, N.J.: Fleming H. Revell, 1984.

Stott, John R. W. *Romans: God's Good News for the World.* Downers Grove, Ill.: InterVarsity, 1995.

Stott, John R. W. *Understanding the Bible.* London: Scripture Union, 1972.

Strobel, Lee and Leslie. *Surviving a Spiritual Mismatch in Marriage.* Grand Rapids: Zondervan, 2002.

Sullivan, Barbara. *The Control Trap.* Minneapolis: Bethany, 1991.

Swindoll, Charles. *Growing Strong in the Seasons of Life.* Grand Rapids: Zondervan, 1983.

Swindoll, Charles. *Strike the Original Match.* Wheaton, Ill.: Tyndale, 1990.

Tada, Joni Eareckson. *Heaven: Your Real Home.* Grand Rapids: Zondervan, 1995.

Tada, Joni Eareckson. *A Quiet Place in a Crazy World.* Portland, Ore.: Multnomah, 1993.

Tada, Joni Eareckson. *Secret Strength.* Portland, Ore.: Multnomah, 1994.

Tada, Joni Eareckson. *When God Weeps: Why Our Sufferings Matter to the Almighty.* Grand Rapids: Zondervan, 1997.

Talbot, John Michael. *The Lessons of St. Francis: How to Bring Simplicity and Spirituality into Your Daily Life.* New York: Dutton, 1997.

Tannen, Deborah. *You Just Don't Understand: Men and Women in Conversation.* New York: Morrow, 1990.

Tchividjian, Gigi Graham. *For Women Only: Keeping Your Balance in a Changing World.* Grand Rapids: Baker, 2001.

Tchividjian, Gigi Graham. *Weather of the Heart.* Portland, Ore.: Multnomah, 1993.

ten Boom, Corrie. *Each New Day.* Minneapolis: World Wide, 1977.

ten Boom, Corrie. *The Hiding Place.* Uhrichsville, Ohio: Barbour, 1971.

ten Boom, Corrie. *Not I, but Christ.* Grand Rapids: Fleming H. Revell, 1997.

Teresa of Avila. *The Collected Works of St. Teresa of Avila.* Trans. Kieran Kavanaugh and Otilio Rodriguez. Washington, D.C.: ICS Publications, 1976.

Teresa of Calcutta. *Blessed Are You.* Eileen Egan and Kathleen Egan, eds. Ann Arbor, Mich.: Servant, 1992.

Teresa of Calcutta. *Love Is Always a Fruit in Season.* Dorothy S. Hunt, ed. San Francisco: Ignatius, 1987.

Teresa of Calcutta. *A Simple Path.* Lucinda Vardey, comp. New York: Ballantine, 1995.

Thatcher, Martha. *The Freedom of Obedience.* Colorado Springs: NavPress, 1986.

Thielicke, Helmut. *The Ethics of Sex.* Grand Rapids: Baker, 1975.

Thomas, Gary. *Sacred Marriage.* Grand Rapids: Zondervan, 2000.

Thurman, Howard. *Deep Is the Hunger.* New York: Harper & Brothers, 1951.

Torrey, R. A. *How to Pray.* Old Tappan, N.J.: Fleming H. Revell, 1900.

Tozer, A. W. *Best of A. W. Tozer.* Warren Weirsbe, ed. Camp Hill, Penn.: Christian Publications, 1979.

Tozer, A. W. *The Divine Conquest.* Wheaton, Ill.: Tyndale, 1995.

Tozer, A. W. *Gems from Tozer.* Camp Hill, Penn.: Christian Publications, 1971.

Tozer, A. W. *High Mountains, Deep Valleys.* Sutherland, Australia: Albatross, 1991.

Tozer, A. W. *The Knowledge of the Holy.* New York: Harper & Row, 1961.

Tozer, A. W. *The Pursuit of God.* Camp Hill, Penn.: Christian Publications, 1982.

Tozer, A. W. *Spiritual Warfare.* Camp Hill, Penn.: Christian Publications, 1996.

Tozer, A. W. *Worship: The Missing Jewel.* Camp Hill, Penn.: Christian Publications, 1992.

Trobisch, Ingrid. *The Confident Woman.* San Francisco: HarperSanFrancisco, 1993.

Trobisch, Ingrid. *The Joy of Being a Woman.* New York: Harper & Row, 1975.

Trobisch, Walter. *Essays on Love: A Reader.* Downers Grove, Ill.: InterVarsity, 1968.

Trobisch, Walter. *I Loved a Girl.* London: Lutterworth, 1970.

Trobisch, Walter. *I Married You.* New York: Harper & Row, 1971.

Trobisch, Walter. *Longing for Love.* Westchester, Ill.: Crossway, 1987.

Trobisch, Walter. *Love Yourself: Self-Acceptance and Depression.* Downers Grove, Ill.: InterVarsity, 1976.

Tucker, Ramona Cramer. *The Busy Woman's Guide to a Balanced Life.* Wheaton, Ill.: Tyndale, 1997.

Tudor, Tasha, ed. and illus. *All for Love.* New York: Philomel, 1984.

Vanauken, Sheldon. *A Severe Mercy.* San Francisco: Harper & Row, 1977.

Vanier, Jean. *The Broken Body.* New York: Paulist, 1988.

Vernick, Leslie, *How to Act Right When Your Spouse Acts Wrong.* Colorado Springs: WaterBrook, 2001.

Von Trapp, Maria. *Maria.* New York: Avon, 1972.

Von Trapp, Maria. *Yesterday, Today and Forever.* Harrison, Ark.: New Leaf, 1975.

Waite, Linda J. and Maggie Gallagher. *The Case for Marriage.* New York: Doubleday, 2000.

Wallerstein, Judith, Julia M. Lewis, and Sandra Blakeslee. *The Good Marriage: How and Why Love Lasts.* New York: Warner, 1995.

Wallerstein, Judith, Julia M. Lewis, and Sandra Blakeslee. *The Unexpected Legacy of Divorce: A 25 Year Landmark Study.* New York: Hyperion, 2000.

Wangerin, Walter. *As for Me and My House: Crafting Your Marriage to Last.* Nashville: Thomas Nelson, 1987.

Ward, Benedicta. *Daily Readings with the Desert Fathers.* Springfield, Ill.: Templegate, 1990.

Ward, Hannah and Jennifer Wild, comp. *The Doubleday Christian Quotation Collection.* New York: Doubleday, 1998.

Ward, Ted. *Values Begin at Home.* Wheaton, Ill.: Victor, 1979.

Warren, Neil Clark. *Finding the Love of Your Life.* Colorado Springs: Focus on the Family, 1992.

Warren, Neil Clark. *The Triumphant Marriage: 100 Extremely Successful Couples Reveal Their Secrets.* Colorado Springs: Focus on the Family, 1995.

Watson, David C. K. *In Search of God.* London: Falcon, 1974.

Weatherhead, Leslie D. *Prescription for Anxiety.* New York: Abingdon, 1956.

Weatherhead, Leslie D. *Salute to a Sufferer.* New York: Abingdon, 1962.

Weatherhead, Leslie D. *Why Do Men Suffer?* New York: Abingdon, 1936.

Weirsbe, Warren. *A Time to Be Renewed.* Wheaton, Ill.: Victor, 1986.

Weiss, Douglas. *Intimacy: A 100-Day Guide to Lasting Relationships.* Lake Mary, Fla.: Siloam, 2002.

Weiss, Douglas. *Sex, God and Men.* Lake Mary, Fla.: Siloam, 2002.

Wheat, Ed and Gaye. *Intended for Pleasure.* Old Tappan, N.J.: Fleming H. Revell, 1981.

Wheat, Ed. *How to Save Your Marriage Alone.* Grand Rapids: Zondervan, 1983.

Wheat, Ed. *Love Life for Every Married Couple.* Grand Rapids: Zondervan, 1980.

Wheelis, Allen. *The Quest for Identity.* New York: Norton, 1958.

White, John. *Changing on the Inside.* Ann Arbor, Mich.: Vine, 1991.

White, John. *The Cost of Commitment.* Downers Grove, Ill.: InterVarsity, 1976.

White, John. *Daring to Draw Near.* Downers Grove, Ill.: InterVarsity, 1977.

White, John. *Eros Redeemed: Breaking the Stranglehold of Sexual Sin.* Downers Grove, Ill.: InterVarsity, 1993.

White, John. *The Fight: A Practical Handbook for Christian Living.* Downers Grove, Ill.: InterVarsity, 1976.

White, John. *Flirting with the World.* Wheaton, Ill.: Harold Shaw, 1982.

White, John. *Friends & Friendship: The Secrets of Drawing Closer.* Colorado Springs: NavPress, 1982.

Whitehead, Barbara Dafoe. *The Divorce Culture: Rethinking Our Commitments to Marriage and Family.* New York: Vintage, 1996.

Whitehead, Evelyn Eaton and James D. *Marrying Well: Stages on the Journey of Christian Marriage.* New York: Doubleday, 1983.

Whitehead, Evelyn Eaton and James D. Whitehead. *A Sense of Sexuality: Christian Love and Intimacy.* New York: Doubleday, 1980.

Whitney, Donald S. *Spiritual Disciplines for the Christian Life.* Colorado Springs: NavPress, 1991.

Willard, Dallas. *The Divine Conspiracy: Rediscovering Our Hidden Life in God.* San Francisco: HarperSanFrancisco, 1998.

Willard, Dallas. *In Search of Guidance: Developing a Conversational Relationship with God.* San Francisco: HarperSanFrancisco/ Zondervan, 1993.

Willard, Dallas. *The Spirit of the Disciplines: Understanding How God Changes Lives.* San Francisco: Harper & Row, 1988.

Williams, Pat and Jill. *Rekindled.* Tarrytown, N.Y.: Fleming H. Revell, 1985.

Wilson, Earl and Sandy; Paul and Virginia Friesen; Larry and Nancy Paulson. *Restoring the Fallen.* Downers Grove, Ill.: InterVarsity, 1992.

Wirt, Sherwood Eliot, ed. *Spiritual Awakenings: Classic Writings of the Eighteenth Century to Inspire the Twentieth Century Reader.* Wheaton, Ill.: Crossway, 1986.

Wirt, Sherwood Eliot, ed. *Spiritual Witness: Classic Christian Writings of the Twentieth Century.* Wheaton, Ill.: Crossway, 1991.

The Wisdom of the Saints, ed. Jill Haak Adels. Oxford, Great Britain: Oxford University Press, 1987.

The World's Great Religious Poetry, ed. Caroline Miles Hill. New York: Macmillan, 1923.

Wright, H. Norman. *Communication: Key to Your Marriage.* Ventura, Calif.: Regal, 2000.

Wright, H. Norman. *Holding on to Romance.* Ventura, Calif.: Regal, 1992.

Wright, H. Norman. *How to Find Your Perfect Mate.* Eugene, Ore.: Harvest House, 1995.

Wright, H. Norman. *The Pillars of Marriage.* Ventura, Calif.: Regal, 1979.

Wright, H. Norman. *The Secrets of a Lasting Marriage.* Ventura, Calif.: Regal, 1995.

Yancey, Philip. *Disappointment with God.* Grand Rapids: Zondervan, 1988.

Yancey, Philip. *Finding God in Unexpected Places.* Nashville: Moorings, 1995.

Yancey, Philip. *What's So Amazing About Grace?* Grand Rapids: Zondervan, 1997.

Yancey, Philip. *Where Is God When It Hurts?* Grand Rapids: Zondervan, 1977.

Yates, Susan Alexander. *And Then I Had Kids: Encouragement for Mothers of Young Children.* Brentwood, Tenn.: Wolgemuth & Hyatt, 1989.

Young-Eisendrath, Polly. *You're Not What I Expected.* New York: Touchstone, 1993.

Zion, William Basil. *Eros and Transformation: Sexuality and Marriage, An Eastern Orthodox Perspective.* Latham, Md.: University Press of America, 1992.

Zondervan Exhaustive Concordance. Edward W. Goodrick, John R. Kohlenberger III, and James A. Swanson, eds. Grand Rapids: Zondervan, 1999.

FOCUS ON THE FAMILY®

Welcome to the Family

Whether you purchased this book, borrowed it, or received it as a gift, we're glad you're reading it. It's just one of the many helpful, encouraging, and biblically based resources produced by Focus on the Family® for people in all stages of life.

Focus began in 1977 with the vision of one man, Dr. James Dobson, a licensed psychologist and author of numerous best-selling books on marriage, parenting, and family. Alarmed by the societal, political, and economic pressures that were threatening the existence of the American family, Dr. Dobson founded Focus on the Family with one employee and a once-a-week radio broadcast aired on 36 stations.

Now an international organization reaching millions of people daily, Focus on the Family is dedicated to preserving values and strengthening and encouraging families through the life-changing message of Jesus Christ.

Focus on the Family
MAGAZINES

These faith-building, character-developing publications address the interests, issues, concerns, and challenges faced by every member of your family from preschool through the senior years.

FOCUS ON THE FAMILY® MAGAZINE	FOCUS ON THE FAMILY CLUBHOUSE JR.® Ages 4 to 8	FOCUS ON THE FAMILY CLUBHOUSE® Ages 8 to 12	FOCUS ON THE FAMILY CITIZEN® U.S. news issues

For More
INFORMATION

ONLINE:
Log on to
FocusOnTheFamily.com
In Canada, log on to
FocusOnTheFamily.ca

PHONE:
Call toll-free:
800-A-FAMILY
(232-6459)
In Canada, call toll-free:
800-661-9800

More Great Resources
from Focus on the Family®

Your Marriage Masterpiece
Discovering God's Amazing Design for Your Life Together
By Al Janssen

Like a long-forgotten work of art, marriage is often undervalued and unappreciated. *Your Marriage Masterpiece* takes a fresh look at the exquisite design God has for your marriage and brings to light the reasons your union was intended to last a lifetime. Throughout this creative and refreshing book, you will examine those elements such as passion, adventure, and commitment that make a marriage a masterpiece. You will be reminded of God's love and passion for you and your spouse, and discover new ways to reflect God's vibrant masterpiece within your marriage.

No More Headaches
Enjoying Sex & Intimacy in Marriage
By Dr. Juli Slattery

As a psychologist and speaker, Dr. Juli Slattery has listened to countless wives tearfully share their hurt and disappointment about their sexual relationships with their husbands. She understands their struggles and the bewilderment they feel. In *No More Headaches*, Juli offers honest answers to the questions wives are afraid to ask. With warmth and compassion, she helps women understand the sexual differences between men and women and offers practical advice for those who want to strengthen—or save—their marriages.

Experiencing God Around the Kitchen Table
By Marilynn Blackaby & Carrie Blackaby Webb

Pull up a chair and have a seat at the kitchen table of someone who has faced life's blessings and its trials. Marilynn Blackaby has often been asked about the challenges of raising five children while her husband, Henry, was heavily involved in ministry and frequently away from home. With grace and humor, Marilynn weaves in lessons she's learned over the years as she shares her personal stories. Marilynn's experiences and wisdom will bring hope and encouragement to your heart.

FOR MORE INFORMATION

 Online:
Log on to FocusOnTheFamily.com
In Canada, log on to focusonthefamily.ca.

Phone:
Call toll free: 800-A-FAMILY
In Canada, call toll free: 800-661-9800.

BPZZXP1